Branding

What You Need to Know About Building a Personal Brand and Growing Your Small Business Using Social Media Marketing and Offline Guerrilla Tactics

Contents

Introduction

One meaning of the word "branding" is the action of marking something, usually cattle, with a hot iron. Ancient Egyptians were the first people to use branding to distinguish cattle from each other, making them less likely to be stolen. While this may seem irrelevant to the marketing-related branding we know of today, it's actually not that different. As time went on, branding became a way for businesses to distinguish themselves from each other in the eyes of consumers.

The simplest way to describe it is by looking at how each business creates a name and design that shows its uniqueness in this vast market. It's not hard to see why branding is a vital process in the lifespan of any business, especially when you see market behemoths like Apple and Google pouring a lot of money into that department.

Branding can be viewed as a promise that a company makes to the consumer, telling them the value or solution they get if they buy its products or use its services. Naturally, different brands cater to different audiences, which allows for a wide range of products and services to prosper. This also means that it's almost impossible for one brand to have it all, whether it's innovation, experience, high value, high quality, or many other brand-defining features.

Branding requires a proper strategy that allows you to contact your potential and existing customers by using the right messages and interactions. The platforms you use for advertising are important to form the right messages. This can translate to what's known as brand equity, allowing a more popular brand to charge more than other brands for a similar product.

The emotional attachment of consumers is a key element in providing value to a company, and since the marketing environment is constantly in a state of change, keeping up with your customers isn't a luxury. Whether you're selling sports apparel or electronics, finding a balance of quality and emotional attachment is essential for your brand to grow.

There is no shortage of branding techniques, but what makes this book different is its comprehensive approach aided by new and updated information to such a complex topic. The book was designed to help new business owners and marketers to not only understand the subject clearly but also to implement it with the least number of hiccups along the way. To ensure that branding can be properly incorporated into any marketing strategy, the latest trends and tools are considered.

Branding isn't just about changing or shaping how consumers perceive your brand, but also how the whole market interacts with it, increasing brand awareness and the overall value of the company. The best recognition a brand gets is when the logo becomes the brand's most recognized element. Whether the logo appears on a physical or digital publication, it should be powerful enough to make a strong impression on the audience the first time.

You'll be able to use branding to increase business value directly since it can establish a leveraged position in the market. This can be easily seen in investment opportunities, as investors will always prefer to go with a company with a favorable public image in the marketplace. As a brand, you should always be looking for growth opportunities, so cementing your position as an established brand in the industry will be very beneficial in the long run.

Good brands can spread between consumers like wildfire. It's not hard to see why brands like Apple are known by almost everyone in the world. Referral business entails new customers acting based on the familiarity and good impressions of other people; once a brand can be seen by the public as something they can trust, a surge of new customers is bound to happen. Once a brand has a favorable position in the industry, the company need not spend as much money on advertising as its competitors. Word of mouth can be an advantageous tool to increase the number of customers as the brand continues to grow. There is no better advertising than the one you don't have to do yourself.

Your employees are also affected by branding, which should help you improve the smoothness and efficiency of the company's operations. Since branding is directly intertwined with the core values of the company, employees who believe in the brand's message will be prouder and more productive because they'll actually feel that they're a part of something bigger than themselves. It's not uncommon for the most successful brands to send the right messages to their employees through various means to give them a sense of belonging in the company.

Customers, employees, shareholders, potential investors, and even distributors should all be on the same page when it comes to an understanding of the brand's message. This reputation is essential to the growth of any brand, ensuring that it has a lot of room to further its relationships with all the elements within the market. No one would want to work for a brand that doesn't represent their personal interests or values.

This book will guide you through the various steps of branding, in addition to explaining how these processes affect your business. Branding is a wide marketing topic, with no one definite strategy that can work for all companies. The book provides a comprehensive overview of the various elements involved in branding, in addition to specifications for implementing the proper strategies to reach the desired results.

PART ONE: Knowing Your Brand

Chapter One: Branding, and Why It's Important

The term "branding" is, unfortunately, used incorrectly in different cases. You might hear people using it when they're explaining logos, slogans, identity design, or even advertising. But you need to understand that this misconception is what makes a lot of businesses, especially small businesses, fail and stray from their purpose. Before I explain to you what branding is, you should first understand what branding isn't. Branding doesn't refer to your products, even though many people say a brand is "product A" vs. "product B." Some people might tell you that a brand is an impression that your product makes, but that only works if you're in the business of selling impressions, and that's not what you're doing, is it? Many people associate brands with logos, and that's incorrect too. A logo is a great tool for any business, and it should be your symbol for the business, but again it's not the brand. So, I want you to read on and understand what branding really is and why you need it for your business.

What is Branding?

To put it simply, branding is a result. This result is what your products, services, or company have created in a customer's mind and how they perceive you. It is that gut feeling in everyone whenever they see your company's name in any product or service you offer. You can't create a brand without your customers, and they are the ones that can elevate your brand to be something great with immense value. You aren't just offering one brand, too, as most people think, but you're giving people millions of brands when it comes to your products because everyone perceives it differently.

Since everyone sees a different "Brand" of your product and services, that means that branding is similar to your company's reputation. Whether it's good or bad, your customers will have different views and opinions on what you're providing for them. Understand that you will get good and bad results, but the main goal is to focus on making good results more abundant than the bad results. This will ultimately be beneficial for your company. You can't get any result without making a claim, promising something, delivering something, reeling customers in with a product, and offering value that is beyond physical attributes. Once you do all of that, the result will be your brand and how people think of you.

Branding is the question you ask yourself about what kind of reputation your products, designs, and messages create. What have you achieved? What kind of effect did it have on your customers? How are all your employees behaving? What is the reaction of everyone involved? And there are a lot more questions involved with the result of your company's products and services. This is why branding takes in almost every aspect of a business. And you need to make sure that the people involved in your small business should affect the brand positively because your reputation depends on it. You don't want anyone hurting the brand and the perception that customers have of you as a consequence. Overall, branding is the feeling of value that goes beyond what you're offering. It's that feeling in customers that helps them choose you over anyone else.

How Does it Work?

Branding works in a way that is dependent on the needs of your customers and clients. So, if you're wondering how your brand will be different, it all depends on the people you're marketing to. This is how people identify you and your product. It's what makes you stand out compared to your rivals and competitors. This is how your customers will distinguish your products and services from other alternatives available to them. But the main goal is to attract them and help their gut feeling lean towards you, allowing them to buy your products and subscribe to your services because they believe that they have made the right choice. You created a product that makes people want to buy it. They want to have it because they know it's the right product for them based on their gut feeling.

This is like the true representation of your business and who you are in the customer's eyes. Your brand is built and elevated by how much people like or love your company and name. But don't give up hope too fast if you're just entering the market with your newly established small business. You can improve your brand significantly by combining a strong message, great customer service, solid promotional campaigns, and a unique logo to top it all off. Once you work hard on all of these aspects, your brand will become stronger and more likable for customers because branding touches almost every aspect of your business.

Why is it so Important?

Branding is important for any business because it can positively impact your company in ways you never thought of. You cannot underestimate the power of people's faith in and perception of you and your company. Branding can literally help your business succeed or fail. The main goal is to achieve greatness, but you need people to see that greatness first and believe that your product and service is better than that of your competition. So, let's explain more about why branding is one of your best hopes for survival and success in the business world.

It Helps You Generate Leads: An excellent brand will make it easier for you to gain more leads that you can later turn into new customers. Referrals and word of mouth will play a major role in this, and it's the best way to spread awareness and gain more customers. Once your business is established, and people perceive you and your products positively, then they will do most of the work for you and start telling their friends and family about your product. People usually go with their gut feeling and spread that feeling to their inner circle.

It Gives You Leverage in the Industry: It doesn't matter what kind of industry you're in because excellent branding can increase your business value. This will give you the leverage you need to succeed in any industry and market because people see you as something appealing and more attractive than the alternative. This helps you to become established in the marketplace. A strong and credible brand will increase that value. Not only that, but investors will want to do business with you. It won't be long until your small business expands and becomes a recognized name that everyone knows.

It Creates Loyal Customers: Loyalty is perceived differently by a lot of business owners, but think of it as people choosing you over someone else. They chose you and will continue to choose you for many years to come because they are comfortable with what you offer. Customer loyalty is needed by any business, and you need for this your newly developed small business. You want people to see you for who you truly are and know they can always count on your services and products to satisfy their needs. This brings in more feedback from other buyers, building your small business, and eventually, your company will succeed and grow significantly.

It Creates Trust: You need trust in the business world, whether it's the customer, employee, client, or investor's trust, a professional brand can showcase your services and products. Trust shows that your company cares about its customers. This is what you should aim for. You want people to trust you and see that you have what it takes to satisfy their needs, deliver quality products or services, and assist anyone with any of their concerns or problems.

Your Marketing and Advertising Campaigns Will Be a Breeze: With a strong brand, your marketing and advertising will go smoothly and effectively. People will see a brand that they know, trust, and perceive as something great. Customers and potential clients will see the strong value that your brand portrays, helping your advertising and marketing campaigns to be strong and impactful. You will be able to create appealing strategies that go hand in hand with your positive brand. This will lead to more awareness, new customers, and stronger relationships with existing customers, increased sales margins, and higher profits.

It Motivates Your Employees: A solid branding strategy will give your employees the push they need to become better. A strong brand is beneficial for your employees because it can help them reach their full potential. They can become inspired by the brand. They know what the company goals are, how to treat clients and potential customers, how to rectify mistakes, and how to succeed under the banner of your company. This is extremely important for small businesses, and you need to train your employees and provide them with the clarity needed to succeed. Their success reflects on your business and your brand.

It Connects with Your Customers Emotionally: A great brand can help you connect with your customers emotionally. This strengthens your customer relationships and your success. Even if you're running a small business, a strong connection with your customers can help you succeed and increase your market share. You will have customers who feel great when they buy your products or subscribe to your services. There will be stronger engagement levels and a positively perceived brand.

What Has History Shown Us Over the Years?

History has shown us all that a strong brand can improve your business. That means that your business is bound to see more success if you work hard on the fundamental aspects of your company. This will help your brand grow, and people's perception of you will only become stronger. Take a closer look at some of the well-known companies and how they're prospering today.

Consider Cadbury. They created some of the world's best chocolates and are loved around the world. But, did you know that Kraft bought the company for almost 20 billion dollars? Do you think it was because Kraft loved chocolate? Did Kraft want Cadbury's numerous factories? Did they want to acquire some of the brightest minds and candy makers? No, the reason behind it all was branding. Cadbury is an established brand, known and loved by millions of people worldwide. Kraft didn't buy a chocolate company; they bought a brand that people admire and trust.

When you look at Disney, have you ever wondered why they bought Marvel Studios? Disney acquired Marvel for 4.24 billion dollars, and it was one of the best decisions ever made by the executives at Disney. They didn't do it because they were avid fans of Marvel movies, it wasn't because they were comic book fans, and it wasn't about expanding away from cartoons. It was about assuming an established and beloved brand that everyone knows and loves. Ever since this acquisition, Disney has prospered, made a lot of money, and succeeded tremendously. This is because the executives knew what the brand offered, and they wanted a strong and credible brand that people love.

You Can Achieve Greatness

Achieving greatness is not impossible, even if you're just a small company or a startup. Having a strong brand can help your business grow, bringing all the benefits of expansion and a larger company.

People look for brands that they trust, and they stick with those brands. Having an excellent reputation should be your goal in the business world. The idea is to help customers and clients see that you are better than your competitors, even though you may both be selling the same products. This emotional attachment, bond, or trust that you can have with your target audience will lift your business, creating a name and brand that will not be forgotten.

It's clear that branding is extremely important for any type of business, whether it's big, small, or a startup that is just entering the marketplace. You need to present your audience with something that has intrinsic value. This is possible if you do the necessary research to understand your target audience and their needs, wants, behaviors, and preferences. Once you get people's attention, and they have tried your products, the branding process will begin. Branding is more important today than it used to be because markets have changed, businesses have evolved, and people's perception of a company can make or break them. You need to build your business in a way that can break the wall of indifference in people's minds. Only then can you hope to achieve a solid brand for your company.

Chapter Two: Knowing Your Audience

The success of any branding strategy in business strongly depends on identifying the target audience and satisfying their needs. Each market offering is specially designed for a particular group of clients. Therefore, it is imperative to know your audience so that you can achieve your set business goals while at the same time satisfying the needs of the target consumers. Knowing your audience helps you conduct market research so that you can keep pace with the constantly changing needs of the customers. This chapter discusses the significance of knowing your target client and the tips you can use to identify them.

How to Identify Your Target Audience

Identifying your target audience is a critical step that can help you build a strong brand that can stand out among the rest. Customers have varying needs and desires, so it is essential to build a brand that can satisfy the clients. You need to identify your customers and understand their desires so that you can build a strong company image. When you know your target market, you can target them with relevant messages and advertisements. There are different techniques you can use to identify your target audience.

Lifestyle

Clients can be segmented according to the kind of lifestyle they lead. A person's lifestyle involves their pattern of living as determined by their interests, activities, and opinions. In other words, lifestyle expresses a person's hidden motivation and value. As a marketer, the concept of lifestyle should tell you why some people buy other products. Certain people buy particular products as a way of showing their status in society.

A good example is that of a person who can move into an expensive suburb as a way of revealing their status. In the same vein, other people, particularly the youth, choose trendy clothing because they believe it will make them stand out from their peers. People create value from different products and services, and this should help you to position your offering to the market. If you feel that your products resonate well with the affluent people in society, then you should make sure that it is valuable.

Age

Another important aspect that can help you identify your target audience pertains to age. While you need not be very particular about individual age, you can try to categorize your target clients into age groups based on generations. For instance, you can target clients between the ages of 25 and 35 years if your company is offering beauty and other trendy products. The youth often identify with fashionable products, so try to identify their needs so your marketing team can design ideal market offerings.

There are also other products that suit the needs of the elderly in different societies. For instance, when marketing consumer products like food and beverages, you need to emphasize the health benefits they offer if your target audience consists of the elderly. It is crucial to identify the trends in age groups among different people so that you can design products that suit the needs of potential clients.

You should also try to establish the stage of life your target clients are in, to design the right products that will satisfy their needs. If the potential clients are new parents, then their needs differ from retirees or college students. Marketers should always know that the needs of different clients are determined by their hobbies and interests during that particular period. These elements change with age, so take your time to learn the behavior of people who belong to a particular niche.

Gender

When identifying your audience, you should not overlook the aspects of gender since it plays a pivotal role in determining your real clients. Other products are gender-specific, so make that clear in your target market statement. For example, when offering skin and other beauty care products, you need to streamline your target consumers so that you target the right group. In this case, you can target working-class females and other potential clients who belong to this category. The same applies to products specifically designed for male clients.

Religion

Establishing your target consumers' religion can also help you understand their needs if you are introducing a new product in the market. This mainly applies to products like foods and beverages since the consumption patterns of different people are determined by their religions. Be honest to avoid violating other people's beliefs since this can jeopardize your brand. And you should not force your brand on the wrong people or try to sneak it onto the market if you are not sure about the value system of the target audience.

Geographical Location

People who stay in the same location are likely to share similar interests in many respects. For example, people who live in a leafy suburb that is also expensive often display similar trends in their lifestyles. These people identify with products with high value as a way of showing their status. In the same vein, if you target people from lower-income groups, you also need to understand how they will perceive your offering.

Usually, people who belong to the same geographical location often share similar interests. This can help you identify the right target clients for your product. In areas where the majority of the residents are college students, they will likely display similar trends in their spending power. Understand the target consumers' specific financial concerns, which can help you set appropriate prices for your products. College students usually like quality, but their spending power cannot be matched to individuals who belong to the working class. This helps to determine the level of income of the target consumers in a particular area.

Cultural Factors

When targeting your market audience, it is vital to remember that consumer behavior is influenced by various factors such as language, social values, and beliefs. Thus, it is important to establish the language of your target audience since this can affect their buying behavior toward specific market offerings. Each society consists of certain values that shape the behavior of its members, and you need to dig deeper to establish these. Some people also have different beliefs that also influence their perceptions of various products offered on the market.

Brand Positioning

When you have identified your target clients, you need to work out a plan about how you can position your brand in the minds of the clients so that it can appeal to their emotional interests. Brand positioning aims to present your product as unique and the best among other similar offerings. Therefore, you need to identify the needs of your target consumers and tailor the marketing message that helps reinforce the importance of your product.

Tell the clients why you think that your product is unique and state what value the clients can get from using it. Marketers of energy drinks emphasize how the products invigorate and energize their users. When positioning the product, focus on the unique features that make it stand out, among others, so that you can appeal to the interests of many clients. Customers may ask if the product adds value to their needs before they decide to purchase it.

Purpose of the Product

To target the right consumers, define the product's core values, and also explain to the target clients why it differs from other market offerings. For instance, you can focus on explaining the benefits and value they can get from using the product. When you launch a product, know that it will not be entirely new since there are substitutes already existing in the market. To gain a competitive advantage, try to position your product in such a way that potential customers will realize additional benefits they can get from using it.

The other crucial thing that you should remember is to give the target consumers assurance about the performance of the brand. This helps to create loyalty among the clients if the brand is aligned towards fulfilling their wants and desires. This can be difficult to achieve, but you need to be honest so that the customers can gain trust from your product. The company's core values can help you clarify what your brand represents and what the users will gain from using it.

Many people are interested in doing business with companies they recognize. Therefore, it is essential to maintain a strong online presence for your brand. Consistently improve your brand and reinforce its values so that the clients can choose it over the products of other competitors. Make sure the brand is easy to recognize.

How to Conduct Market Research about Customer Preferences

When you have defined your target audience, it is crucial to understand their needs. You can do this by carrying out market research, helping you to identify the right potential customers. The markets for different products consist of diverse people from various backgrounds, and their needs significantly differ. Therefore, you must use appropriate strategies to research the needs of different clients before you roll out your product. You can try the following methods to gain insight into what the customers may want.

Social Media Analytics

Social media is increasing among different people who connect with their friends and relatives in different places. Enlightened companies are harnessing different social media platforms to market their brands. The most common social media platforms include Instagram, Twitter, Facebook, Pinterest, LinkedIn, Brandwatch, YouTube, Snapchat, and many more. Companies can carry out marketing campaigns showcasing their products, and clients, in turn, can use different features such as comments, likes, shares, clicks, and video views that are found on different social media platforms. You can use the data you gather from your social media accounts to improve the performance of your brand on the market.

There are both free and paid social media analytics tools that you can use to analyze data about clients. Likewise, sustained social media marketing campaigns around your brand are likely to bear positive results if they are meaningful to the targeted audience. You need to tailor the message about the brand so that it appeals to the emotional interests of the clients. You can test your social media adverts to check how the target clients respond.

Word of Mouth

When launching a new product on the market, direct interaction with potential clients can help you identify their needs and wants. Word of mouth is very powerful since it helps you to explain the product features and its benefits to the consumers. The other advantage is that the consumers also get the opportunity to try the product before they purchase it. Customers are likely to buy a market offering if they have an idea about how it functions. Many people are likely to buy products they think can make a difference in their lives.

The success of any business strongly depends on several factors that make the organization's brand stand out among the rest. To achieve this, you need to know your target audience so you can satisfy their needs. It is essential to begin by identifying different factors that influence the buying behavior of the consumers so you can offer a unique product. Effective branding helps create the identity of your brand, which in turn helps to appeal to the emotional interests of the consumers. If you are offering a new brand, you need to define its purpose along with the benefits that can be obtained by consumers by using it. When you know the needs of the consumers, it becomes easier to position your brand in the right marketplace.

Chapter Three: Service Brands vs. Product Brands

Businesses offer either products or services to their clients. When you are in business, make it clear to your target clients about what you offer. This distinction helps you design an effective branding plan that can help create an identity for your brand, either as a service or product. Brand recognition helps customers identify with your business, which contributes to its success. A brand is the most enduring asset of the firm and makes it stand out among other competitors. This chapter discusses the difference between offering products and services. It also explains the branding strategies that can be used when marketing products or services since they are different.

What is a Product?

A product is defined as anything that can be offered to the market for acquisition, attention, use, or consumption that may satisfy the user's wants or needs. A product is tangible, and it can result in ownership after acquiring it. A product is physical in appearance, and you gain ownership of it. You can also keep a product for future use since you can store it in a safe place.

While products also represent more than tangible goods, products mainly encompass physical objects, services, places, persons, organizations, and ideas. The term product is broad, but this chapter pays special attention to tangible products. It explains why branding strategies for physical products differ from intangible services.

What is a Service?

A service is described as any activity, satisfaction, or benefit offered by the other party and is intangible. Paying for a service does not result in ownership of anything. For example, if you go to the bank, you receive a service, whereas airlines and hotels also offer services. Using these services does not result in ownership of anything, but you do get satisfaction, which you cannot see, test, hear, or hold.

The other key feature of a service is its inseparability, which means services cannot be separated from the providers. The provider who offers the service immediately becomes part of it with the customer. Thus, the interaction between the customer and the service provider is crucial since it affects the outcome of the service. The quality of the service also strongly depends on who provides it. For instance, other airlines or hotels provide better services than other players in the same field. Another feature of a service is that it cannot be stored for later use or sale. If you miss your appointment or flight, you need to rebook, and this can come with additional charges.

A firm's market offering includes both products and services, and it brings value to the users. The firm's offering becomes the foundation upon which the company tries to build profitable relationships with their customers. During the current period, as both products and services are commoditized, many businesses are increasingly moving to a higher level in creating value for their clients. To differentiate their market offerings, companies are creating branding strategies meant to improve customer experiences. The next section focuses on branding strategies for both products and services.

Branding

A brand is a name, sign, term, symbol, or design that helps to identify the maker or seller of a particular product or service. It differentiates an organization from other competitors in the market. Thus, branding is the art of influencing the consumers' perception of a product, service, or organization. If properly utilized, branding helps improve the visibility of the company and the products and services it offers.

The major notable aspect of branding is that it has become so strong in the operations of any business so nothing can go onto the market unbranded. However, for branding of products and branding for services, some differences exist. Know the differences between the two concepts if you are concerned about the viability of your business in the long run.

Since products and services are different, this means that the branding process between the two cannot be the same. When designing your branding strategy, know that it cannot be universally applied to both products and services. The following are some factors that can influence your branding strategy for a product or service.

Product Branding

If your business offers products, then your branding strategy should largely focus on visuals. For instance, you can focus on fonts, product photography, and visual branding, and these are mainly designed to help make your product visible on the market. Beautifully designed and presented visuals appeal to the feelings of the people who will get a glimpse of them. This will also compel potential clients to try the product when they see it is appealing.

Essentially, when branding a product, you aim to appeal to the emotional feelings of the customers, so they can choose it over other offerings. The main advantage of branding a product is that the process is easier than branding a service. It is easier for the clients to experience the product before they get hold of it. A customer can analyze the image of the product, and they see all the features that can help them make an informed decision when it comes to purchasing.

Product branding uses real images which help the consumers to focus on different features that can help them try the product. When a customer decides to buy the product, they may not have it from the day they purchase it. Therefore, when branding a product, make sure that the customers have a feel of it so they know the value and benefits they can get from using it.

Use of Audio Stimuli

Branding of products can also involve the use of audio stimuli. For instance, you can use catchy tunes that appeal to the interests of the clients so they can try the market offering. This strategy also helps to fulfill the needs of other potential clients with visual challenges. Audio stimuli should always focus on the positives of the brand so as to appeal to the interests of the customers. Tailor the message so that it suits the needs of the target clients.

Story Telling

Storytelling is another effective method that can help you develop your brand. You can share articles about your product and tell potential clients what they should expect from using it. It is also important to educate people about the product so that they will buy it fully knowing what they will get from using it. Focus on the visuals so, when you design the message, it is simple and easy to understand. People will be more interested in what they see, so the product design should be top class. As you will see below, branding services are mainly concerned with creating trust between you and the target clients. This makes the two strategies quite different.

Service Branding

Branding services, on the other hand, aims at building trust and mutual relationship between the marketer and the target group. Since a service is intangible and cannot be stored for later use, it should have immediate results. This helps create trust among the clients if they know that they will get the satisfaction they crave from using a service. In most cases, it is impossible for the client to feel the benefits of the service long after they have left the place.

All the same, you should practice what is commonly referred to as long-term branding. Even if the clients cannot see the results immediately, convince them to trust your offering. To convince the clients about your offering, you should focus on service delivery. For instance, you can focus on aspects such as good customer service and convenient services that are unmatched. If you are operating in the aviation industry, emphasize the quality of service delivery.

Thus, the major difference between product branding and service branding is that the former mainly focuses on visual stimuli. Branding for the products normally aims to create a lasting impression among the clients so they can hold the product in high esteem. The strategy involves the use of catchy images and tunes to reinforce the importance of the brand compared to other similar offerings on the market. Both audio and visual stimuli help to attract customers to a particular product.

But service branding mainly focuses on creating trust among the target clients and showcases the benefits of the offering. Clients cannot hold services like they hold products, but they should be satisfied with the offering. Therefore, you need to convince the clients you offer better services compared to the competitors.

Building Strong Brands

Remember one very important thing as you go about your branding of products or services. Branding is about presenting a positive profile for the entire organization. Branding makes your company different from other competitors in the eyes of your customers. Focus on the reputation of the company so people can recognize and connect with it for their needs. This makes branding beneficial for your business since it allows you to stand out amongst the rest of the other actors. Therefore, it is vital to create a strong brand since it is more valuable than the assets of the organization. The following strategies can help you create a strong brand.

Brand Equity

A brand is more than just a name or symbol since it plays a pivotal role in creating and maintaining the firm's relationships with its customers. A brand represents the consumer's perception and feelings towards the performance of the product. Thus, the real value of the brand is its ability to capture and retain consumer loyalty and preference. This is also called brand equity and describes the customers' positive differential effect of knowing the brand name, and their response to the service or product offered. Brand equity can be measured by the extent to which customers will be willing to pay more for the brand compared to other offerings. Loyal customers will go the extra mile, and they pay a premium for their preferred brand.

Build a Strong Brand Name

The success of the product on the market strongly depends on a strong brand name that encompasses the product and its benefits. A strong brand name should resonate with the target clients so they can identify with it always. This helps create loyalty among the target consumers, and they will look no further than your brand because they hold it in high esteem.

Brand Positioning

Effective marketers position their brands in the right place in the target customers' minds. They can position the brand in such a way that the customers can associate it with the benefits they will get from using it. Strong brands are usually positioned according to strong beliefs and values attached to them by the customers. The brand position offers a consistent promise to deliver certain features and benefits to the clients. This helps the consumers to identify with their chosen brand.

Creating a brand strategy for products and services is similar since you aim to identify your target market in both cases. You also aim to analyze the competitors while generating brand attributes that will make your product or service stand out among the rest. However, your strategy will have a different focus on services and products. Product branding primarily focuses on using beautiful visuals that are aimed at attracting customers to your products. But service branding aims at creating trust among the clients for the services offered since these cannot be owned like products. The bottom line is, branding helps to create an identity for the product, and it helps it stand out among the rest.

Chapter Four: Brand Image and Identity

Many people use the two terms "brand image" and "brand identity" interchangeably, but while they are interconnected with each other, they are different. In simple terms, brand image is a metric used to show how people perceive a brand. But a brand identity is the concept of image that a specific brand has about itself, aspiring to become by implementing various techniques. The two marketing concepts, brand image and brand identity, are intertwined. No business can achieve the brand identity it has in mind without considering the status of its current brand image. Various techniques are implemented by businesses to assess brand image accurately, besides strategies that allow a brand to carve the image it wants.

Increasing Importance of Brand Image

Brand image always has been important, but it seems that, as technology progresses, it's becoming more important than ever. Consumers have many more options than they used to have, which means that competition between brands is getting heated when it comes to market domination. A business shouldn't just add to the background noise that distracts consumers when they're buying something, but instead, it should be the first thing a consumer thinks of when they're ready.

Customers nowadays aren't interested in buying from the brand that sells the best products or services. Rather, they're looking for the brand that they can trust in terms of morality, support, and quality. Consumers may find a brand that shares similar values to theirs as the perfect brand to buy from, even if there are many others who may have similar qualities. This means that consumers can switch between brands in an instant if they find a brand image that they can get behind.

While brands are only organizational entities, the image that people can have of a brand is mainly an emotional one. The best brands are those who make sure that their brand image conveys positive key values it has. This overall impression on consumers is developed from numerous identifiers and associations which brands provide.

Brand's Image and Impression

Making a good impression in business can translate to success in the world of business. Consumers can judge your brand and create their first impression from factors like the dress code of employees, website, organization of retail store, design of the package, and many other similar factors. While it may seem superficial at first, it's these factors that can easily influence consumer's opinions of your brand, especially when a lot of brands provide similar products or services to yours.

Even basic things like business cards can show your potential customers that the brand has a strong eye for detail and style. While customers don't deal with a brand just because they have good-looking packaging or business cards, it's things like these that can create a memorable impression imprinted in a customer's mind.

Recognition of a Brand

You can take some brands of today as an example. No one mistakes the apple logo behind Apple devices, the BMW insignia, the colored Pepsi logo, and many others. While it may seem like a simple feat, it's actually a hard one, with millions of dollars poured specifically into helping consumers recognize a brand.

Even though those logos are well-designed and accompanied by great mottos, it's not really the only element that allows the widespread recognition between consumers. A brand image has to portray efficiency, quality, and speed through visual means and business-based interactions. Brands should focus on creating a consistent image that appears throughout their interactions with potential consumers and existing customers.

The type of business may affect the techniques used to create a recognizable image. Service-based businesses that don't sell physical products tend to focus on customer relations and long-term support of the services that they provide. Product-based businesses tend to outline their products' image with their values and company culture through other indirect means.

Image and the Portrayal of Structure

You don't really want to visit a store or a restaurant where you have no clue who to talk to because no one is wearing name tags or a uniform. No matter how much better the quality of services or products provided by a business, if consumers are confused because they can't identify who to turn to for help, they won't leave the store happy. No matter how efficient or smooth the operation of your store is, without a polished brand image, it's hard to convey such good qualities.

You don't want potential customers to think that the business is still trying to learn the ropes. Things like professional email addresses, uniforms, and business cards can make a huge difference in how customers perceive the organization and professionalism of your business. Simple and easy steps to make your business look put-together and structured can be often overlooked in the pursuit of harder goals, which ends up backfiring on the brand image.

The Effect of Brand Image on Credibility

Successful brands focus on portraying a credible image for their customers, increasing their loyalty and trust. Providing the right services or products at the right quality might not be enough for potential customers to trust your brand. The consumer's relationship with your brand is one of the main elements that allow the growth of your brand. A brand's promise that is delivered perfectly to the consumer leaves a very long-lasting impression of the credibility of your brand.

The goal of building credibility is to have your potential customers think about the core values of your brand when they're considering their options. Consumers are looking for brands they feel like they can trust. Since it's hard for someone to trust a brand they have never purchased from before; brands have to focus on creating a credible image that can easily show trustworthiness to consumers.

The Definition of Brand Identity

Many new entrepreneurs may struggle to find the brand identity that best suits their brand. And since brand identity is exceptionally important in creating a proper brand image, its elements must be considered and planned. Your brand identity is how your brand expresses itself, from the trademark to the logo. Your brand's visual appearance, interactions, and portrayal are all important elements of establishing a brand identity.

Creating a unique brand identity is one of the most recognizable ways to stand out from the competition. It also allows creating new experiences that increase the tendency of consumers to engage with it. While some brands manage to create artistic expressions of their identity, like Apple and LEGO, a lot of brands find it difficult to perfectly communicate the brand identity they have in mind.

To avoid falling into branding pitfalls, it's important to understand the main components of a brand identity's core values. These foundations are essential in determining the position of your brand in the market, in addition to how it can differentiate itself from other brands.

The Values and Mission of a Brand

The creation of the core values of a brand is one of the most important concepts that should be thought of early in the process of establishing a brand. Your mission, values, and vision are going to be your compass in defining the experiences you offer to your customers. The actions of your brand should always be in sync with its core values and vision. No matter how recognized or successful a brand is, being inconsistent with their established values can spell their downfall.

Your employees' engagement is affected by the mission and values of your brand. You are not only looking to attract consumers but also attracting top-performing employees who truly believe in the core values and vision of the brand. It's much easier to establish a brand identity when the majority of your employees are in sync with what the brand offers. This isn't only important for brand identity, but also the productivity and performance of employees.

Brand Positioning Statement

Just like it sounds, brand positioning means the occupancy of a brand in a specific or unique place in a consumer's mind. This is an essential tool used by any brand to stand out from the crowd. There are some tactics and strategies involved that can help a brand take the right path and guarantee its uniqueness.

The brand positioning statement is vital in creating or building a proper brand identity. They aren't slogans or mottos used by the business in ads or billboards; it has more to do with the internal vision of the brand and how it can be used to arrive at a competitive position in the market. The statement can be thought of as inspirational, but it has to be grounded by reality to allow strategizing.

1. **Consumers:** Focusing on the target audience you've decided to market to, which means being relevant with sound judgment about the type of products or services they are interested in. It hinges on the balance provided by mixing features and attributes with benefits, and finally, the needs of the consumer.

2. **Competitors:** The positioning statement should factor in competition to help focus on specific claims that allow the brand to find a place for itself in the market. It involves researching competitors to find what consumers look for, and then creating a founded plan.

3. **Business:** The positioning statement has to be within reason to allow the brand to deliver it through interactions with consumers reliably without inconsistencies. The more the positioning statement can be incorporated into the aspects of business, the more valuable and recognized the brand becomes.

Brand Personality and Target Personas

You may have never heard about it, but every successful brand has a unique personality, just like humans do. It was designed to instill some sense of humanity in brands to bring it closer to consumers, which beats the cold and harsh numerical nature of the market system. These personalities also help brands distinguish themselves from competitors. If you're trying to create a brand personality, think of it as having a voice of its own, in addition to other humanistic characteristics. A list of the most prominent attributes your brand has should help you discover what your brand has and what it lacks. A brand personality helps you properly market to the target audience in a consistent manner.

After you've delved deep into the attributes of your brand, you need to find out what the target audience wants from you. A marketing message without certain consumers or target audience in mind is a weak message. You may need to get a little bit on the technical side and look for demographics and psychological factors to determine your best target audience. You can also categorize your target audience into 3 to 5 personas to help you factor in variations between consumers.

Elements Involved in Designing Buyer Personas and Surveys

After segmenting the broad target audience into smaller groups, it's wise to use them as starting points for basing target or buyer personas on. You can approach the customers of each segment directly by conducting interviews or sending surveys, and by the process of elimination, ensure that the groups are laser-focused in terms of variety. It's common for brands to use research panels for each group that combines different budgets, demographics, business size, and other relevant variations.

You can base your surveys on a few key elements that ensure you get a deep understanding of your target audience. Start with product concepts that customers either need or would like to have, so you can prioritize product development and marketing accordingly. It's easier to incorporate modification surveys that help you fix products or services already in place, which will help you know your points of strength and weakness.

You'll want to analyze the data you collect to be able to follow trends and even predict them. You can even use your sales figure to augment the thoroughness of your analysis and its conclusions. Your personas should be easily relatable from an individualistic standpoint, a theoretical model person for each persona. The more detailed the persona, the stronger your ability to make business decisions will be. Focus on background information, personal hobbies, interests, goals, the relatability of your brand, and any objections to what your brand offers, which will help you create detailed personas to target.

Brand Identity and Consumers' Needs

Consumers are only interested in a brand or business because it solves a problem. Whether the company is selling fire alarms or e-books, it's helping consumers in their hunt for convenience or even survival. The focal point of your brand identity is the solution to problems that consumers are having. The brand identity has to be clear and direct when it comes to addressing a problem and its solution to the consumer. Whatever it is that a brand may offer, it's imperative that it makes it as clear as possible to consumers.

Important Brand Identity Features

Since the brand identity is a common element between all those who are related to the brand, whether employees or consumers, a strong brand identity ensures that everyone is on the same page. There are some common features of strong brand identities.

- It has to stand out from the brand identity of your competitors, especially the biggest ones.

- Incorporate visual elements that help customers recall it easily when seen, and it doesn't even have to include the brand name, as we've seen with Apple.

- Your brand identity should have enough leeway to allow the scaling and growth of the brand

- It should be as clear as possible so that employees can implement it in their work easily

Common Branding Mistakes

Branding can be a pretty sensitive marketing phase that not all companies manage to navigate without losses. It may help to learn from the most common mistakes made by other brands.

- **Lack of Consistency**

If you really want to keep the brand image in the clear as a brand, you have to be consistent with the messages that your brand sends out to consumers. It's easy to focus on one aspect of marketing while forgetting other less important ones, which ends up drawing a messy portrait of the brand image.

- **Uninformed Employees**

A lot of companies fall into the pitfall of keeping their employees in the dark when it comes to brand identity. While most executives or high-tier employees may have a fairly good understanding of the core values of the company, they can fail to deliver that message to their employees. Employees should be trained while having a clear understanding of what the brand stands for.

- **Old Marketing Materials**

In the internet age, marketing is evolving at an unprecedented phase. Using old marketing material may have been a viable option in the pre-internet era, but nowadays, many marketing techniques can become obsolete overnight. It's important for a brand to stay updated with the latest marketing techniques to help form the image that they have in mind.

PART TWO: Building Your Brand

Chapter Five: Your Branding Strategy

The success of any business depends on how consumers values their brand. If you want to build brand equity or add value to your company, there are many branding strategies in marketing that you can adopt. It is essential to build value for your company from the consumers' perspective. Some organizations employ different branding strategies to increase their brand equity. This chapter explains what branding strategy is and various steps that can be taken to build a strong brand. The chapter also outlines the step by step approach that you can take in the branding strategy process.

What is Branding Strategy?

The brand strategy aims to promote the specific and long-term goals of the company that makes it identifiable in the market. Essentially, every business aims to generate revenue and ultimately profits from its operations. This can only be achieved if all operations of the business are aligned towards the satisfaction of consumer needs while at the same time aiming to gain a competitive advantage over other players in the same industry.

First and foremost, you should know that your brand is not your product, name, logo, or website in the case that you offer a variety of products. A brand is more than that since it represents an intangible feeling and separates your firm from the rest of the competitors. Therefore, to keep your business viable for a long period, you need to adopt a strong brand strategy. The following section outlines some of the branding strategies that you can adopt for your business venture.

Branding Strategies: How to Build Strong Brands

Brands are valuable assets to the organization that should be carefully developed and managed. A brand is more than just a name and symbol; it is a key element in the company's relationships with its consumers. However, branding often poses some challenges for marketers. This section examines key strategies that can be implemented for building and managing brands.

Brand Equity

A brand is more than just names and symbols since it represents the firm's relationships with its clients. A brand represents the consumers' perceptions and feelings about a particular product and its performance. Thus, the real value of strong brands lies in their capability to capture and retain consumer preferences together with loyalty. In some cases, consumers bond well with specific brands, which can be attributed to high brand equity. When a customer's response to any particular product or service has a positive differential preference caused by the brand name, we call that brand equity.

It basically adds value to your company. Look at it this way; some people are more willing to pay a premium for the brand of their choice. The main reason behind this is that they perceive their preferred brands to be more valuable than other products on the market. Likewise, many people often associate high prices for different brands with high quality, and this is exactly why they pay more for specific brands.

High brand equity offers the firm many competitive advantages. Powerful brands often enjoy high levels of consumer brand awareness and loyalty. A powerful brand also represents a set of profitable and loyal customers who are ready to defend their brand preferences. Consumers always expect to gain more value from their brands, and they remain forever loyal.

Brand Name Recognition

The product's success can be attributed to a good name. However, it is challenging to find the best brand name. Finding a brand name often begins with a review of the product, together with the benefits that the target clients can get from using it. Some of the good qualities of a brand name include the following:

- It says something about the product's features, benefits, and qualities

- A good brand name should be easy to recognize, pronounce, and remember (simple is good)

- Quality brand name should be distinctive

- A good brand name should be easy to translate into other languages

- It should not infringe on other existing brands

When you have selected the right brand name, it should be protected. Many established companies often try to build brand names that extend to their products. For instance, brand names that include Colgate, Vaseline, and Tupperware, among others, have succeeded in this way. Additionally, most companies with large brand name recognition are also recognized by elements such as logo, colors, or slogan. Companies like Apple, Starbucks, Coca-Cola, and Mercedes-Benz quickly come to mind. These iconic companies also feature multiple subsidiary products under the company name. A brand should help consumers identify the company and its products.

On top of creating a strong brand name, you should also emphasize the purpose of the brand. While all brands promise something to the clients, you should go the extra mile by defining the exact purpose of your brand to help it stand out among the rest. Your brand should reveal some willingness to offer more benefits to the clients instead of just fulfilling your profitability goals. You can achieve this by defining the functionality of the brand and what the consumers will benefit from using it.

Position Your Brand Correctly

You should position your brand clearly in the minds of the target clients. When you position a brand, you should focus on the product attributes and desirable benefits that the clients can get from using a specific product. You also need to put emphasis on the mission and vision of the brand when you position it. The firm promises to deliver the clients certain features and benefits to the consumers. To win the hearts of the consumers, ensure that your brand promise is simple and honest.

Most brands are positioned based on the strong beliefs and values associated with them. Therefore, when positioning a brand, aim to appeal to the emotional interests of the target clients so they can also share the same vision with you. Usually, consumers need to be convinced about the value and benefits they will get from using certain benefits. You should present your brand as having attributes that make it valuable and unique from other offerings.

Private Branding

The other strategy that can help you build a strong brand is the use of private labels, also called store brands. Private brands are now very common in large retail supermarkets. For instance, large retail chains like Wal-Mart, Pick n Pay, Kroger, and Food Lion, among others, offer cost-effective brands, and these compete with brands offered by other large retailers. It seems many retailers are offering store brands, and these compete with other established brands at all levels.

The main advantage of private brands is that they are relatively cheaper compared to established brands. Consumers who are budget conscious usually find store brands affordable, and this helps the retailer to generate more revenue from the sales of these brands. Private brands also carry the supermarket's logo, and many clients will identify with the organization, which helps build trust and loyalty among them. Private brands also give retailers the flexibility to pack what they want on their shelves at any given time.

Brand Extension

Brand extension, as the term implies, helps extend the current brand name to other new or modified products in the market. If you are into shoemaking, you can also extend your flagship brands to include jackets. The main benefit of brand extension is that it gives your new products instant recognition as well as quicker acceptance. The main reason for this is that the customers already identify with the existing brand name so they will readily accept the new offering if they are loyal.

Creating loyalty among the customers is very important since it helps the firm to have a strong customer base. It also saves the company high advertising costs that may be required when it is building a new product. Brand extension can also help your company to gain a large market share as it diversifies its market offerings. When the other product portfolio fails, the company can capitalize on the other products available. However, when extending your brand, remember that it should not divert from your core business. Many people often identify with the core values of the organization, so try to avoid introducing a completely different product line from your current portfolio.

Consistency

When branding your product, you should always be consistent with the key features and benefits that it offers. You should avoid talking about certain things that do not enhance your brand. When communicating, align your message to the brand and avoid confusing terms. You need to ensure that your messaging is cohesive and will consistently help to build a strong brand. This, in turn, promotes customer loyalty.

Consistency enhances brand recognition, and this is very important since it helps to attract more customers. For example, you can look at how Coca-Cola's marketing strategies are all directed towards presenting it as a reputable brand that is designed to satisfy the needs of the clients. When marketing a brand, the other important thing is to avoid falsehoods about your offering. You would rather be honest and state clearly what your product promises to offer.

When customers are still new to the product, they are curious, so provide them with reliable information that can help them develop some trust in your brand. They will likely try the brand when they realize that it promises features that can satisfy their needs. However, if your brand is premised on falsehoods, you are likely to scare away the customers, which can impact its image negatively.

Appeal to the Emotions of the Customers

Another effective branding strategy that you can adopt is to appeal to the emotional interests of the target clients. Not all customers are rational when it comes to buying different products. It is not surprising that one would prefer to pay hundreds of dollars to buy a particular product while they can still get the same for a relatively lower price. This is where you should focus on appealing to the emotions of the buyers.

People often need to build a sense of belonging to different companies that offer a variety of products. It is easier for the clients to identify with a specific brand than everything they can get from the market. Therefore, you should aim to appeal to the emotions of the customers so that they can develop a strong liking of your brand. People usually display a physiological need to be connected to others so that they can form a strong bond and relationships. The customers can even defend the premium prices that you will offer on your products.

Thus, if you are concerned about building a strong brand, you need to connect with your clients on a deeper level. Make the clients feel like part of your family since this helps to foster a strong relationship and loyalty. It is advantageous for the company to have a strong base of loyal customers that can ensure its viability in case of unprecedented changes in the market.

Attracting customers to your brand is good, but building loyalty is a critical element of every successful brand strategy. It is easier to retain the customers that you already have than attracting new ones. Therefore, if you strive to build loyalty among them, you are likely to promote a positive relationship between your company and the existing clients. Loyal customers can also attract new clients, which is a bonus for your business.

Stay Relevant

Businesses operate in an environment characterized by constant changes; hence, the organization must remain relevant in its operations. This calls for marketers to be creative in their campaigns so they can keep pace with the changes taking place in the environment. Be flexible in your marketing campaign so your company can set the preferred standard for your brand.

When your branding strategy is flexible, you can make necessary changes that can make a difference. Positive changes to your branding strategy help build interest and differentiate your brand from that of your competitors. A flexible branding strategy involves new packaging, a strong online presence, and new product names that will draw the attention of many potential customers. For the brand to be identifiable, it is crucial to roll out new marketing strategies to keep it fresh in the minds of the clients.

The trick here is that you should not fear change. If you realize that your old tactics are no longer working in your favor, it is high time you change strategy. You can try to engage your followers in a way that helps invigorate their perceptions about the brand. If there are new attributes to the brand, then you can use them to connect with both old and new customers so that it remains relevant in their minds.

Know Your Competition

All businesses operate in competitive environments, so you should aim to gain a competitive advantage at whatever cost. Other players in the same industry are also be competing for the same customers, so you need to design a winning strategy. It is essential to take competition as a challenge that can help you improve your overall brand. For instance, you can achieve this by researching how other competitors operate.

This helps you design a unique branding strategy that cannot be easily copied by your competitors. If you know the tactics used by your competitors, then you can react quickly should some changes take place in the environment. A great way to improve your brand is to constantly learn different things that can affect its overall presentation on the market. Uniqueness is vital if you want to sell more of the same products that are also offered by your competitors.

Employee Involvement

The success of different branding strategies also depends on employee involvement in the decision-making process. Your employees need to be well versed in how they should communicate with the customers. To achieve this, you can incorporate their ideas and views into the company's overall brand strategy so that they can also develop a sense of belonging.

When you treat your employees as viable assets to the company, they will meaningfully contribute to the decision-making process that can affect the brand. Likewise, you should always know that highly motivated employees are more productive and can positively contribute to the success of the company. To win the hearts of the employees, you should ensure that they also share the same vision and core values of the organization and can easily identify with it.

As you have observed from the above aspects, effective branding plays a critical role in determining the success of your brand on the market. A quality branding strategy is beneficial for your company as it helps to promote long term goals that make your brand identifiable on the market. It is crucial to align the operations of your business towards the satisfaction of the target clients while at the same time aiming to achieve your desired goals.

Chapter Six: Your Online Presence

When you are doing your research on how to build your own brand, you will notice that your 'online presence' is mentioned in all branding guides and online articles that you come across. Given an integral part, the digital component plays in the success or otherwise of your brand; it seems only befitting. The way you approach social media platforms and the way you present your brand from the tone you use and the content you share will all determine how the public perceives your brand and the business behind it. Although it might seem like a challenging mission, especially if you are not familiar with the basic concepts of online branding, it could actually be the right outlet for you to be able to compete with the bigger brands. Many small businesses have cleverly carved their own unique digital spaces and took their once unknown brands to levels they could have never possibly imagined. Whether you are a new business owner and want to make sure you are giving your business the best chances to succeed, or perhaps you are just curious about this buzz-worthy topic, this book is for you. Here you will find out how you can build your online presence and how to best utilize it to maximize its potential. Let us get started.

What is Online Presence?

First things first, before we dig deeper into the subject of online presence, let us first define exactly what it is. Your online presence refers to how you use the internet to introduce your brand and help your target customer know about your products' existence. This includes your social media pages, your website, as well as any other presence online like blog posts. It is important to note that any mention of your brand that customers can find online when researching certain keywords will be part of your online presence even when you do not have control over it, which makes it that much harder to maintain. That being said, being present online will open new doors to your business and give you the chance to maximize your reach to get new customers in simple ways, like reading about your business featured in an online magazine.

Apart from reach, you should learn about the other numerous advantages that your small business could gain when you build a strong online presence. Here are some benefits.

To Be Able to Stand Up to Your Competitors

Unless you are operating in a very niche market, chances are you have a lot of competition. There seems to be too much of everything across all price points, and, being a small brand starting up, you can become easily discouraged by this. However, the only way you can stand your ground and challenge your competitors is to focus on your online presence. Although they probably have their own strategies, try to do it in a better way. Identify your target audience's most used keywords when searching for similar products, so you can make sure you appear at the top of the search result page (more on that later). You need not spend a fortune, but you can find a good website developer to develop your website and make it aesthetically pleasing and user-friendly. While fancy websites can be quite attractive, they can also be intimidating for consumers to browse through, try to avoid this mistake, and simplify the navigation process for your customers.

At the end of the day, it is all about driving sales, so if you have a website that is doing this efficiently, then you are on the right path.

Collect Valuable Customer Feedback

Having an online presence will give you the chance to collect real-time feedback from your customers and act accordingly. If, for example, you were thinking about adding a new product to your hair care line, instead of wasting money that you cannot afford to lose, you can easily construct a poll and ask for your customers' opinions. You can gain valuable insights about whether it will be a good idea, and if so, at what price point and what other important features that your customers care about. This will ensure that when you do decide to release the new product, you are almost certain that you will have enough demand to make it profitable.

Make Virtual Sales

Whether you start your own brick and mortar or decide to sell exclusively online, having an online presence will allow you to literally operate around the clock. With your online shop being accessible to all your customers around the world, one could be placing an order in the morning, while another can be placing theirs late at night when it is still afternoon on your side of the world. Without having to put any actual sales effort, your website can be working for you from day to night. As a small business, this can be like a dream come true, having your website flooded with orders while avoiding hefty overhead costs of operating an actual store. You can use this relatively fast money to reinvest in your business and grow it further.

Humanize Your Brand

Although we have come a long way since the dawn of the digital age, people are still wary about getting involved with brands that seem to be run by machines. Customers of today want their chosen brands to have a human voice. When they are asking for after-sales support, they want to feel like they are speaking to someone instead of getting automated responses. Your online presence will allow you to connect with your customers in new ways. You will have the chance to develop a trusting relationship with your audience to encourage them to engage with your brand and continue sharing the word and promoting it.

Give Your Brand a Voice

Many brands have succeeded in using their online presence to gain their own voice. Think about how the brand name, Toms, is associated with giving back to the community and supporting the less fortunate. The footwear moguls are one of the most famous brands to use the "One for One" model, where they donate one pair of shoes to a child in need anywhere in the word for every pair they sell. Toms uses their social media platforms and website to propagate this message over and over until it has become synonymous with the brand name. Your online presence can enable you to find your own voice and maximize its potential. By using your online pages to reflect the light in which your brand will be seen, you will be able to build a stronger brand that can withstand the fierce competition.

Now that we have established how online presence can do wonders for your small business, let us move forward to the "how" part? When you are starting from the ground up, how can you go about building your online presence to start reaping its benefits? While there is no one single answer to these questions, there are many tools that you can use to fulfill this quest.

Understand the Importance of SEO

Search engine optimization or SEO is a vital tool that you have to master when building your online presence. When you learn how SEO works, you will be able to guarantee the visibility of your website to potential customers who are looking for products similar to yours. By doing some research and learning how to read simple analytics, you will be able to identify the keywords that are often associated with products like yours. If, for example, you run a small health and wellness business, some keywords will be obvious like health, wellbeing, and yoga. Those, however, can be quite generic, and you will want to dig deeper to find less-common words. Through your research, you can unearth other more targeted words like "Ayurveda" and "Homeopathy." Including these new keywords throughout your website pages can boost your position to the top of the search result page, which will, in turn, increase traffic on your website and eventually maximize sales and profits.

Use Email Marketing

Email marketing can be a great way to connect with your existing customers and reach new ones. Whenever new visitors browse through your website, ask them to provide you with their email addresses. This emailing list can be of great help to reach out for feedback about your customers' sales experience and getting the word out about your new store. It is worth mentioning that you have to make your emails relevant and meaningful. Do not bombard your recipients with redundant information and expired deals. Instead, help them see the benefit they are getting from your email blasts. Email marketing can also help you reconnect with old customers who have been inactive on your website for some time. For those, you can send a 10% discount for returning customers, or something along the same lines. Make your emails sound friendly and fresh, so that your customers will be eager to open new emails from you instead of sending them straight to the spam folder.

Make Social Media Work for You

You cannot deny the power of social media. People who were once skeptical about its role in generating sales and driving businesses will now vouch for its worth. Do not just create social media pages and sit down to watch what will happen. Instead, you have to adopt a creative and active approach when handling your socials. Through some market scanning efforts and diligent research, you can find out what your target audience is following on social media. The kind of content that is receiving the highest interactions and sharing is where you will want to invest your time and money. If your product is aimed toward young females and you want your brand to sound relatable, you can start creating content that young women will find interesting; fun posts about dating tips, career advice, and wellness can all be good topics. Seek collaborations with other brands that your audience finds exciting and will want to follow their new projects. By associating yourself with the right names and hashtags, you will strengthen your existence in the realm of social media and all that it has to offer. Try to remain true to your brand and how you want to be perceived; this will prevent you from pursuing the wrong partners and influencers. Make it a point to focus on your target audience, pay attention to the small cues, like the initiatives they are supporting, and then try to imagine new ways you can relate to them. One golden rule is no matter which strategy you decide to follow with social media, be consistent. If anything, social media is all about being in the moment and keeping up with the fast-paced digital world.

Try to Find New Online Spaces

Granted, this might sound impossible, but if you are taking your research work seriously enough, you might be able to strike gold. Imagine if you were one of the early adopters Instagram for business and all the biggest brands on the planet followed in your footsteps, pretty exciting, right? By keeping an eye on online trends and your consumers' behavior, and with some experience, you will be able to tell which new apps are bound to become the next big thing. Not only will you always be celebrated as one of the first players, but you can also save a lot of money in subscription fees that websites and apps start to apply once they become popular.

Put Out Meaningful Content

Valuable content is king when it comes to online branding. Your product can be of great quality and deliver what it promises; however, how easily your target customer can reach you is what can make or break your business. By creating meaningful content, you increase the probability of having your posts shared across different platforms and even going viral. People like a brand that can use its website to share interesting and informative content that they deem worthwhile of their browsing time. Do not just use your website and Facebook newsfeed to repost the few reviews your customers left years ago, use that space to start new and exciting conversations instead. For example, if you are a small acupuncture clinic, you can fill your online pages with interviews with prominent sports figures naming the ways acupuncture has worked for them and improved their performance. Although the topic has to eventually be related to your business, it does not have to be the only thing you discuss online. Put yourself in your customers' shoes and identify what content they would find appealing and can provide the highest engagement rates. Always keep value at the back of your mind when you are working on your next blog post, and, over time, you will fortify your online presence.

Foster Meaningful Relationships with Relevant Influencers

Over the last decade, influencer marketing has caused a lot of controversies. While some brands remained hesitant to hire influencers to drive their sales, many others have jumped on the wagon head-first and are so glad they did! Looking at how powerful and established influencers have become, as businesses seeking an online presence, you cannot pass on the opportunity of finding the right ones to work with. People follow thousands of influencers on Instagram and other apps to see what they are wearing, brands they swear by, and others that they cannot live without. Wanting to have similar experiences like their favorite influencers, followers take their words and buy whatever it is that they are selling. Unlike signing up celebrities to promote products, people view influencers as regular people, and therefore their lifestyles are more attainable than the actors who make millions of dollars in income. Within a short period, you will see how using influencer marketing can hugely improve your image online. However, if you want to use influencer marketing to build your online presence, you have to find the right influencers that promote the same image that you would like your brand to identify with. If you work in the sports industry, reach out to influencers who are known for their athletic backgrounds and their love for sports, so that you can get the right message out about your product without seeming to be only after money, when you are researching the influencers market. Try to be as specific and as goal-oriented as possible. No matter how big an influencer is, if she/he does not fit your profile, then there is no point in reaching out.

Online presence is no longer a nice add-on to your offline existence, but rather it is a necessary complement to make sure your small brand has a better chance to enjoy exponential growth. Do not be discouraged by the many acronyms and numerical data that goes into building your brand online, with some trial and error; you will be able to make it all work. Continue reading the next chapters of this book for more eye-opening information about the vast world of branding and the many ways it can help your budding new business.

Chapter Seven: Online vs. Offline Marketing

Even though online marketing has taken a colossal leap and overshadowed offline marketing, which was once a leading paradigm for most brands, you can still consider appointing both forms of marketing to promote your business. However, you might face far-reaching questions such as, which is more effective? What kind of results can I expect? Is it specifically advantageous for my brand niche?

To answer these questions, let's dig into details and envision the potential of online and offline marketing in this chapter. In the end, we will also discuss the approach that is more suitable for your brand.

Online Marketing

Online marketing involves the promotion and advertising of your company's campaigns, messages, and content with the aid of digital tools. There are several online platforms to leverage your marketing game. Your target audience is placed online, mainly on social media channels. This placement can be fueled by a mutual presence between your brand and your ideal clients, luring them towards your landing page. It is mostly based on a click-bait approach. With the rapid rise of digital tools and services, online marketing has pushed offline resources and taken a permanent form of promotion for a majority of brands.

Pros and Cons

Pros

- The biggest benefit of online marketing is its cost-effectiveness. All you need is a stable internet connection and an efficient device to produce content and float it online. At most, you'd have to spend on online digital marketing strategies that include technical aspects such as SEO, PPC, etc., which are actually quite cheap when compared to offline marketing.

- Spread word instantly. Whether you are uploading content on social media or using pay-per-click ads, you are just a mouse-click away. The speed and convenience of online marketing let you spread the word as soon as you apply the strategy. And, of course, you get to enjoy the results for a longer period.

- The advent of digital technology lets you measure and analyze your marketing performance with ease. Some of these tools direct your ads to a specific audience based on the demographic and geographic factors of your ideal audience group.

- Tools, such as Google Analytics, display real-time results after running an online marketing strategy. You can learn from the amount of engagement and preferences of your customers and frame your strategies accordingly for a more successful campaign in the future.

Cons

- You need to invest in online tools and devices. For online marketing to work, you have to depend on technology. If you are not versed with tech, it could take some time for you to actually begin marketing.

- Most users, including you, scroll past ads and completely ignore them. Unless you display an ad or content that's a bit unconventional, it'd be difficult to gain attention.

- The market is saturated. Since most brands are using online marketing and creating an online presence at an exponential rate, there is too much competition. You need to stand out or be different to garner attention from your customers.

Useful Online Marketing Strategies

1. Social Media Marketing

Social media presence is one of the top online marketing strategies that your brand or marketing agency has to adopt. In today's digitally driven world, social media presence is of utmost importance. Billions of people use social media platforms on a daily basis, such as Facebook, Instagram, Snapchat, Twitter, YouTube, etc. Most of these media provide an opportunity to create the content of varying forms - images, videos, stories, and text. Target your audience and narrow down to two or three platforms that are the most suitable for your business. Create accounts on each and post alluring content to mark your digital presence. We will elaborate further on this in the next chapter.

2. Establish Lead Magnets

Lead magnets refer to a situation in which you, as your company's head, offer your services or some valuable piece of content or information in exchange for their contact details (mostly full names and email addresses). This can be done by asking them to subscribe to your blog by providing their email address and receiving a valuable e-book or informative PDF in exchange. You can also put up an ad or a download link on your website that directs your audience to the free document. Use these contact details to follow up on your potential customers.

3. Use Retargeting

Retargeting is when you are showing your ad to your ideal target audience and directing them to your website or landing page for further inquiry. For this, the users should have previously engaged with your content in some form. This is how retargeting works- when a user arrives on your landing page, you can conduct frequent follow-ups that might make them increasingly interested in finally trying your product or service. With higher frequency, you are establishing more trust. The beauty of retargeting is that you can direct your users from various social media channels to your landing page or vice versa using the same ad, making it an omnipresent marketing strategy.

4. Content Marketing

By creating content and presenting it to your audience, you can build an authoritative rapture within your niche. Among several forms of content such as videos, podcasts, interviews, blog posts, etc., you need to choose a form and style that you are most comfortable with. If you are still confused, you can opt for videos as your main form of content, which gives way to a sub-category called video marketing. Videos are the best form of engagement, as most users prefer to watch videos to learn about a subject when compared to reading articles or listening to audio guides. By creating videos, you can also extract snippets for your blog posts, prepare audio guides, and run your social media channels.

5. Define your Target Audience

This strategy involves defining your ideal customer to understand what they want and prefer, particularly from your brand. Consider a few factors in crafting your ideal customers such as demographic details (age, gender, occupation, and income bracket), psychographic details (hobbies, likes, interests, opinions, affiliations, and beliefs), and geographic details (location, neighborhood, city, state, and country). These details will provide a clear picture and a definition of what and how your ideal customer should be. By defining your customer, planning your marketing strategies will get much easier. You will know which social media platforms to target, which campaigns to launch, and how new products will resonate with the mass population. This will truly assist in running your marketing game.

6. Use Search Engine Optimization

SEO is another boon for online marketers. This mechanism allows the search engine to filter and present content based on the keywords and relevance of any user's topic of interest. By using SEO, you can push your page to the top rankings of relevant search results. This is directed in two ways - on-page and off-page search results. On-page results are mostly based on the keywords used in titles and subheadings of any blog post, article, or published content. Off-page rankings are governed by the type, quantity, and quality of any content. Dedicate a part of your budget on tools for SEO.

Offline Marketing

As the name suggests, offline marketing involves promoting your brand's content and reaching your target audience without the help of the internet and online tools. Some of these strategies and media involve newspapers, radio, business cards, etc. Before the advent of online marketing, companies were thoroughly embedded in offline marketing tactics for more than two decades. However, offline marketing still thrives due to its numerous benefits.

Pros and Cons

Pros

• Offline marketing can fetch trustworthy clients that are willing to do long-term business with you as compared to a one-time client with online marketing. However, this won't always be the case. All we are saying is that the chances for this occurrence are higher.

• One-on-one interaction is often enough to lure someone into doing business with you. This shows the true and human side of your brand, which most clients are able to trust. At times, you can convince someone with a few words where hundreds of adverts may fail.

• Offline marketing provides tangible promotions such as products or brochures. Your customers will have something to hold on to, which will constantly remind them of your brand.

- You can build some valuable life-long relationships. Having important contacts is necessary in the business world. This is beneficial for both your personal and professional life.

Cons

- Since offline marketing deals with television commercials and newspaper ads, it'd require you to spend a huge chunk of your budget to create brand recognition. Along with sending emails and calling individual clients, strategies such as TV and radio commercials are the only means to reach a larger audience at the same time, which might demand a huge sum of your budget.

- Offline marketing might take a longer time to fetch leads and earn more profits.

- The exposure is limited. With offline marketing, you are targeting clients on an individual level with no guarantee of them returning to you. This can become dreary and exhausting. Offline marketing isn't for you if you don't have enough patience.

Useful Offline Marketing Strategies

1. Carry and Distribute Business Cards

Oh, the good old' business cards. They can never go wrong. While carrying and distributing business cards might seem like a long shot, this strategy certainly reaps results in the long run. Whether you are attending a business event or simply fetching groceries, make sure to keep a few business cards with you at all times. You can meet a potential client anywhere and at any moment. Slip them under doors, slide them under newspapers, stick them on public bulletin boards, or hand them to people in the waiting room during your doctor's visit. Do not miss any opportunity.

2. Get in Touch with Your Local Publication

A feature in local or national magazines, newspapers, and publications can instantly catch people's eyes. Contact your local newspapers and print houses to have your work featured. Whether it's a submission, commission, milestone, or a paid ad, try your best to be featured. While you are at it, ensure that the magazine is directed toward your target audience. This will increase your chances of gaining more clients in the long run. Publish ads related to important events hosted by your company to make people aware of their occurrence.

3. Keep Track of Trade Shows and Fairs

Trade shows are an optimum way to gain maximum target clients. Since these shows are aligned towards a specific niche, you can also study your competitor's whereabouts and learn several tactics to run your business. By participating in trade shows, you are literally putting your products or services out in the market. You get to advertise your brand, study the competition, unearth new strategies, and gain clients. It's an absolute win-win ploy.

4. Consider Rebranding

By rebranding, you are partly or entirely changing the look of your brand and product. This can include tweaking your logo without losing its significance, switching to a contemporary color palette, or revise your product's packaging. By applying these changes, you are presenting a new face with an old soul to your customers. Many companies have deployed this rebranding strategy and were quite successful. A few notable examples are Taco Bell, Instagram, Mastercard, and Pandora, among many others. However, this step could backfire if adequate planning and contemplation aren't implemented. Consider this step only if your brand has been in existence for a while and if it actually needs a new identity.

5. Host or Sponsor an Event

Host an event to celebrate your company's milestones or employees' achievements now and then. Invite influential people and the local press if the event is conducted on a large scale. This is a great advertising tactic to reach out to people and eventually gather more leads. If you have the luxury, sponsor events that revolve around your niche. This is what major brands are doing. By sponsoring important events, they have the freedom to display their products and establishing a positive brand image.

6. Consider Public Speaking

Even though public speaking isn't your strongest suit, this can be an effective marketing tactic to mark your brand's recognition in the market. This will not only increase your brand's reach, but you will also get a massive opportunity to build a like-minded community. Keep track of events within your niche and try to take part as a public speaker. Some events might keep you from self-promotions, which might, in a way, affect your brand's marketing. Find ways to subtly promote your products or services in such instances.

7. Send Mail

Unlike email campaigns, this is an old-school approach that might demand a massive chunk of your marketing budget but is highly effective in establishing important connections that tend to last. Print brochures, gift coupons, newsletters, and company magazines, and send these to old clients, acquaintances within your radius, and potential clients. You can also send product samples and ask for honest feedback. In this way, you're not only fetching more leads but also gaining perspective on improving your product. If possible, try to personalize these prints and samples before sending them as people will appreciate it for your thoughtfulness. This will, in turn, instigate your old and new clients to spread the word and get back to you for business.

Which is More Suitable?

Well, it's simple. It will majorly depend on the type of business you run or the purpose you want to fulfill. Both online and offline marketing hold specific benefits and disadvantages that can be advantageous to your company. Since online marketing costs less money and produces long-term results, you can definitely switch to this medium to market your brand. However, do not underestimate the ability of offline marketing to drive sales. This tool has the wherewithal to bring value to your brand. Even if your brand is dealing with e-commerce, which is entirely based on digital platforms, you can still incorporate offline strategies to market your services.

With an affluence of budget, you should include both online and offline marketing strategies in your game plan. If you are flexible, you can try both game plans and incorporate the one that works more effectively. It also depends on your niche. For instance, fashion and beauty niches can work both online and offline. All you need to do is find the sweet spot after a few trials and errors. This is also necessary to finally fetch the balance between online and offline marketing for your brand.

To achieve this balance, you can also merge these arenas by creating a symbiotic relationship. Who says we can't use both, right? For example, you can use online tools to analyze offline data (like the success of events or number of clients that can be expected in your store), urge online customers to visit your store or convey your social media or website details through business cards, brochures, and public speaking.

Experiment your way towards success with a few hit-and-miss tactics, and we are sure that you will find the medium that works for you.

Chapter Eight: Social Media Marketing

Since we mentioned social media marketing in the last chapter, we will have a broader look at it here. You will gain answers to questions like - Why is social media marketing so important? How can it benefit my brand? How can I implement it?

As you already know, and, as the name claims, social media marketing is marked by marking your online presence across substantial social media platforms. However, many uninformed brands fail to unleash the potential of social media marketing. It's more than just creating an account on Instagram and posting content. You need to dive deep into analytics, set certain goals, collaborate with people, maximize engagement, and create and post valuable content.

The importance and value of social media marketing have made it a necessity for all brands instead of being an option. This chapter will cover all the necessary aspects of social media channels (benefits, effective strategies, and individual platforms) and how you can make maximum use of these to promote your brand.

Benefits of Social Media Marketing

Massive Target Audience

Whether your company works for car rentals or sells handmade cosmetics, you can always find your target audience on various social media channels. Platforms such as Instagram, Facebook, YouTube, Twitter, and Snapchat (among many others) collectively host billions of active users. It's a massive sea to catch some like-minded fish.

Inexpensive

Social media is a free tool for everyone, irrespective of their identity, background, and operational discipline. Creating and signing up is free. With time, you might have to dedicate a small part of your budget for promotions or to buy tools that provide an in-depth analysis of your social media performance. However, these costs are relatively low when compared to other forms of digital marketing.

Blank Canvas

Social media platforms offer a blank canvas on which you can post various forms of content- images, text, video, stories, etc. This is a great opportunity to be as creative as you can - there is no limit. Collaborate with content creators, create IGTV videos, produce comics, the options are endless. It's a great way to explore your creativity. You can also learn about current trends and get inspired by innovative ideas.

Integrity

Most of these media are integrated with each other. In a wider sense, you can link your accounts and direct your users from one platform to another. With this integration, you can also cross-post your content on multiple media at the same time. Even though cross-posting should be avoided, you can still add important events and make your followers aware of it through all platforms. For instance, Instagram is owned by Facebook, which allows all brand accounts to be linked with their pages on both media. This makes handling and operation much easier.

Better Engagement

Social media is all about engagement. You get the opportunity to hold real-time conversations, ask questions, and reply to your followers individually. And, increased engagement is a boon for your brand. Platforms such as Instagram and Facebook let you host live videos, which produce maximum engagement. Stories, Direct Messages, and comment threads are other extensive interaction tools.

Effective Social Media Marketing Tips

1. Know Who You Are Talking To

Since you are already familiar with the term 'target audience' due to its consistent use in the previous chapters, you can easily understand this tip. Basically, you need to figure out your target audience by determining who you are talking to. This will not only determine your suitable target audience but also assist in formulating your marketing strategies. Now, learning about your audience is essential to most types of digital marketing strategies, but it is more important for social media. Why is this?

First, you no longer have to scratch your head to come up with ideas on producing content. With a defined audience, you know what they'll like and what will be unacceptable. You can easily build your content plan around these people with a belief in achieving success at the earliest.

To know who you are talking to or interacting with, use these pointers to make a quicker analysis.

• Keep constant interaction by replying to comments, answering DMs (Direct Messages), and updating stories.

• Use the insights and analytical tools that are available in most of these platforms to decipher the age, gender, nationality, and time of interaction of your audience.

● Extract their pain points. Whether it's an issue with your product or unsatisfactory customer support, dig into the problems of your audience and build your next strategy or campaign around it. But first, try solving related issues.

● Get feedback from your followers. Ask questions within captions of your post or spoon-feed them with content based on your surveys and questions. You can also use stories to understand your audience.

2. Define a Set of Objectives

Do you want a wider customer base? Do you want to drive more sales? Or are you just aiming to build more recognition? Define a set of goals that you want to achieve with social media marketing. This will assist you in framing your strategies effectively. It is unwise to produce content and start posting it across platforms without defining your objectives first. To give you a fair idea, most small businesses expect 70% lead generation, 53% brand awareness, and 50% customer engagement from their social media marketing strategies. Your reasons and objectives might vary, which is why defining them is necessary to gain a clear direction. A few companies also look forward to providing better customer service through social media.

3. Pay Attention to Your Content

Your content will determine whether your followers decide to stay on your page or not. If you fail to engage or entertain them, all it will take is a click to unfollow or unlike your page. Produce content that is interesting, informative, or entertaining. Make sure that your content isn't too promotional. Ephemeral content typically stays for around 24 hours and disappears, which makes it a short form of engagement for most of your followers. Stories are considered to be ephemeral content, which can be found on platforms like Instagram, Facebook, and Snapchat.

Another important aspect is your consistency. Even if your content is engaging, you might lose followers if you don't post consistently. Posting one post a day is the best consistency rate. However, refrain from posting more than 3 to 4 times a day as it could spam your followers. Even if you have some important content to display, use stories to deliver your message.

As mentioned in the previous chapter, video content produces maximum engagement and is the most organic way to fetch followers. Since most of these platforms, mostly YouTube, are video-centric media, you can upload and distribute your content quickly. Pay attention to stories, live videos, and images also.

If we get into the specifics, try creating one or more of these content types to offer versatility to your audience:

• Create personalized content. This form of content will be relatable to most of your audience due to the displayed sentiments and indubitably beckon them to stay connected to your brand for a longer period. For instance, brands that design jewelry often construct videos around wedding proposals that evoke emotions among their customers.

• Induce humor. Humor is the best form of engagement and entertainment. Wit and clever humor, if incorporated within your content, is bound to make your audience chuckle and stay connected. Brands like Burger King and Old Spice constantly produce witty campaigns that garner their audience's attention.

• Engage your audience in live videos and stories. Live videos are real-time conversations that can be streamed on channels like Instagram and Facebook. Your audience can like, comment, and ask you questions. Stories, specifically on Instagram, have several interaction-inducing features such as polls, Q 'n A's, and quizzes.

• Create more behind-the-scenes videos. This is the best way to display the 'human' side of your brand. Help your audience realize that a lot of hustle and hard work goes into the perfect presentation they see and access every day. This will develop trust among your followers and compel them to keep following and buying from your brand.

These are just a few ideas to get your boat floating. Depending on your brand type and niche, you can create exclusive content that's user-centric. Stick to what resonates with your audience. The bottom line is, create more engagement and interaction with your followers as it will turn your leads into sales and presence into recognition.

4. Try UGC or User-Generated Content

User-generated content is essential to your clients' buying decision as it is directly related to your clients' buying experience. Around 88% of US customers rely on their acquaintances' reviews before making an important purchase decision. Not only that, 81% of customers would buy a UGC-approved product instead of buying a similar product that's cheaper but has no reviews. Another important factor that makes UGC a relevant marketing tactic is the ability to build brand awareness. A new customer will trust the word of an existing customer, which is beneficial for your brand identity and lead-generation.

5. Run Contests

Platforms like Instagram are apt for running contests, which develop a wider follower-base and assist in gaining valuable brand recognition. You need only to assign a set of products or gift cards as rewards and ask your existing users to spread the word to win.

This is how you can effectively run contests:

● Set the final objective of your contest. You can easily frame your contest depending on the expected result - more followers, more sales, or wider brand awareness.

● Choose an apt social media platform to run the contest. To decide, reflect on factors such as the number of followers, larger target audience, and tools.

● Frame contest guidelines such as the deadline, prize, and tasks.

● Create a post that resonates with your brand identity.

● Spread the word.

The most common type of contests (also effective) are giveaways in which the user is asked to follow and tag three friends. The winner is picked randomly.

6. Consider Influencer Marketing

The rise of social media over the past 5 to 7 years has led to a massive surge in influencers and bloggers in various niches, most notably within beauty, fashion, food, travel, and lifestyle categories. Influencer marketing gels well with social media as all influencers use a platform to establish their online presence. As the name suggests, these bloggers 'influence' people by providing useful tips and showing them the right way to live.

Most brands want to hire major influencers with a huge follower-base. They expect to fetch more leads and followers for their own brand through this tactic. But let us tell you a secret, the true ability to get potential customers lies with micro- and mini-influencers. Even though these bloggers have fewer followers when compared to major influencers, they have a stronger connection with their audience. Their reach is smaller but stronger. Also, partnering with 10 micro-influencers will still be cheaper than paying one major influencer. However, if you are easy on the budget, you can hire influencers on all levels.

The rise of influencer marketing is dawning upon small brands, and 67% of them are already on their feet with expanded budgets to include influencer marketing. Also, influencer marketing has a 28% online customer-acquisition method, which gives you another reason to include this strategy within your game plan.

7. Determine a Suitable Social Media Platform

Since there are several social media platforms to choose from, you should analyze each and stick to two or three to market your brand. Let's take a look at each one of these and filter the most suitable option for your brand. Your social media marketing plan will only be successful if you use the right platform for your brand.

This brings us to our next topic of discussion.

A Brief Peek at Platforms

Among several social media channels, you should study and incorporate one or more these potentially relevant media.

Facebook

Facebook has been the most popular platform for over a decade. 86% of all social media channels and small businesses use Facebook due to its versatile demographic presence. Facebook also accumulates around 1.5 billion active users daily, giving you a major chance to catch your target audience. One exceptional tool is Facebook Groups. It provides a personal space to interact with your followers and answer their questions, which, in turn, increases engagement.

Instagram

Instagram gathered fame and sky-rocketed over the last five years, so much so that it is clicking shoes to become the top social media platform in all areas. Instagram has introduced a number of features over the years. It started off as a curator of images from personal lives, more like an online album, with users posting pictures of their food, childhood memories, and travel shenanigans. But, with its rising popularity and addition of valuable features, it steadily became an important business tool. You can now post stories, conduct live videos, post IGTV videos, and image-based content. Business and shopping tools are additional attractions on Instagram. You can add product details within your content that directs the concerned user to your landing page to complete the shopping.

Snapchat

Directed mainly towards young adults and the Gen Z population, Snapchat is rawer when compared to other social media platforms. This medium is based on stories as its main form of content. These stories disappear within 24 hours of floating and, thus, give you enough flexibility and freedom to create coarse content without much pressure. One major attraction of Snapchat is its AR filters that enable engagement. If your main objective is to establish a true connection with your audience, Snapchat can be your go-to platform. Create behind-the-scenes videos more often or engage your audience with personal or team interviews each week.

Twitter

Twitter has made its way on the list of the top social media platforms in 2020. As of 2019, this platform churns around 6,000 tweets per second, totaling up to 500 million tweets in a day. With more than 320 million active users, Twitter is popular among small businesses due to its excellent customer support facilities. It offers the freedom of holding real-time conversations and better communication opportunities through Twitter Chats and building a like-minded community.

YouTube

Along with being a major social media channel, YouTube is also one of the biggest search engines that churn millions of videos, in and out. With the advent of smartphones, a majority of users have switched to YouTube's mobile app. We also have YouTube stories now, which, unlike others, stay for 7 days.

Apart from these major social media platforms, you can consider channels such as LinkedIn, TikTok, and Pinterest if any of these resonate with your brand. LinkedIn is directed towards professional B2B connections, TikTok is suitable for companies that want to retain a whimsical identity, and Pinterest is more image-centric and suits visual content.

PART THREE: Growing Your Brand

Chapter Nine: Building Brand Awareness and Trust

Now that you have learned strategies to get the word out there about your brand and the best ways to use the online and offline marketing tactics to your benefit, you want to make sure you become a brand of choice. You want your customers to continue coming back without feeling like they need to think twice about it. This, in a nutshell, is the power of building brand awareness and trust that will eventually translate into customer loyalty. Trustworthy brands turn into household names that remain relevant throughout the generations. The ultimate goal of most brands is to become the Coca Colas and the Carriers of their category, where they no longer have to compete to sell. Instead, their consumer-base has become sturdy enough that it is only getting bigger over time. The way you price your products, deal with your customers, and handle problems will all affect the extent to which your customers can trust you. The more open and transparent you are, the greater your chance to strengthen your relationship with your customers. In this chapter, you will understand the importance of brand awareness and trust and how they affect the growth of your business. You will also learn about the different tactics and insightful tips on how you can build brand trust so you can put the theoretical information into actionable strategies. Let us dive right in.

How Brand Awareness and Trust Affect Your Growth

As a small brand, the way you can grow your business is to create a certain image in the minds of your customers. Once you establish yourself as a solid brand, your existing customers will happily refer you through their own networks; this will boost your sales and grow your business further. Especially in this digital age, one good review from a satisfied customer can enhance your brand image and vice-versa. Thanks to the internet and social media platforms, information travels within a matter of seconds, so you will also have to act fast to preserve your volatile growth. Focusing on building your brand awareness will make it much easier for new products you introduce to succeed since they will be backed by an already established brand that customers know and trust. However, some of the common beliefs that the consumers have towards business entities make this process more difficult. All businesses exist to profit, so to shift your consumers' attention away from this and make them see that you are on their sides and have their best interests at heart is quite a challenge. Let us move forward to identify the tools that you can use to achieve this seemingly impossible task.

Different Techniques to Build Brand Awareness and Trust

• **Adopt a Transparent Approach When Dealing with the Public**

People appreciate honest brands that are not afraid to admit making mistakes and then act to correct them. Disclosing information about where you source your raw materials and your production process will make consumers believe that you have nothing to hide. Shady businesses that choose to operate in the dark often find themselves subject to public backlash even if they were running a clean business. Consumers want to take a look inside your business; this is especially true for sensitive products like food and personal care items. A great example to mention here is how McDonald's' cleverly handled the controversy it was caught in a few years ago. When some parents and nutrition experts started a campaign against the fast-food giant, questioning the hygiene of their kitchens and the freshness of their raw ingredients. McDonald's decided to arrange daily tours and brought their consumers in to see for themselves how the food is prepared. They had nothing to hide and found a smart way to put the rumors to rest once and for all. Involving your customers and being as open as you can be will help your brand to be viewed as a respectable and trusted brand.

- **Provide Exceptional Customer Service**

When treated right, customers develop an affinity towards any brand. You need to focus on creating the ultimate customer experience from the minute the customer steps foot into your virtual or physical store. Make great customer experience a core mission of your business and make sure all your staff reflects this ethos in the way they work. If you have an online store, focus on making the browsing experience simple and hassle-free so that your customer will want to recommend your services to others. This will show that you value and respect your customers and want to make sure that you are providing a consistently efficient service. Collecting meaningful feedback from your customers and keeping an eye out on market trends will help you find out what your target customers are looking for and what they would identify as a great customer experience. The key to making this happen is to have a dependable quality control system in place to alert you whenever corrective actions are needed.

- **Be Picky About the Partners You Choose to Work With**

The companies you choose to befriend and have your brand's name associated with theirs will have a huge impact on how much your consumers will trust you. You need to carry out extensive research before agreeing to collaborate with another brand. You have to first collect info regarding your target audience's impressions about this other company and then assess how beneficial this partnership will be for your business. Even if it seems like a great opportunity, the data you collected from your customers could suggest otherwise. If so, you should pull the plug on this collaboration and continue searching. Alternatively, when you work with other brands that your customers respect and think highly of, this will further prove that your brand is legitimate and deserves their trust. Keeping an open channel with your target customers will direct you towards the right partnerships.

- **Follow Your Customers' Preferred Channels**

This is especially important if you are targeting the younger generation. Making your consumers see that you are trying to connect with them through favorite platforms will help them appreciate and trust your brand. Young people today value brands that can speak their language and can adapt to the digital existence that they chose for themselves. To reach your customers, you have to use your social media platforms to introduce new marketing campaigns and shed light on new products. Through your research, you can find out where your target audience is spending most of their time and follow them there in a creative manner. If there is anything younger people dislike, it is being 'fed' information in an old-school way and feeling like they are being tricked into making a purchase. The best way to avoid this is to remain informed about the new trends and continuously studying your customers' behaviors.

- **Be Responsive**

If your brand becomes known as the brand that 'responds,' then you are more than halfway towards building brand trust. Just like in real life, the response is the minimum act of decency when someone addresses you. Attending to your customers' requests and inquiries promptly will let them know that they are being heard. Regardless of what kind of reviews your customers leave on your website's feedback section, you have to make sure you acknowledge each and every one and takes any necessary actions. Try to go above and beyond. When someone leaves a complaint about delayed delivery, apologize and, next time, offer free shipping to make it up to them. Being one step ahead and nimble with your responsiveness is reason enough to make your customers, both existing and potential, decide on your brand over your competitors'.

- **Show the Faces Behind Your Brand**

Today more than ever, consumers are more interested in the human-factor behind their favorite brands. Consumers have been dealing with intangible brand names for so long now, that there is a serious yearning to highlight the human aspect in the business world. There are many interesting ways to let your customers see the personal side of your business. For example, you can film your story as a young entrepreneur who had a dream and worked hard to make it happen and post it on your Instagram page. You can also use your website and social pages to introduce your team to the public, show them that Mary, who handles your product development, loves dogs, and that is why she made sure your products are cruelty-free. Or, create YouTube vlogs to show what a typical day on your premises (no matter how small) looks like. Even something as small as signing people's names at the bottom of emails can make your brand more personal. These stories and small gestures make a brand more approachable and can greatly help in building the trusting relationship you are seeking with your customers.

- **Stay Consistent**

If you want to have a trusted brand, you cannot have double standards when you are a business operating in the public eye. If you have built a wide customer base because of having certain political standings, you cannot shift the next day and support the political campaign of an opposing party. Your customers will view your inconsistency in politics as a lack of commitment to certain standards and values. They will suspect that this might as well apply to your quality standards and all other aspects of your business. You should also reflect consistency in your brand's name, logo, and design. Not only will this improve your brand awareness, as people will be able to differentiate your brand from among others, it will also impact your brand trust. Maintaining consistency is one of the basic ways to gain someone's trust and keep it.

- **Provide High-Quality Product**

This, of course, will depend on the resources you have access to; however, you should always make sure that you are providing your customers with the best quality you can produce. Your product is the central pillar on which your whole brand exists; while it is vital to pay attention to everything else around, your product is your bread and butter. If your customers see that you are doing a great job with your customer service and maintaining transparency and honesty, yet ignoring the quality of your product, your brand will come crumbling down. Spend your first years in business perfecting your product and, once you have that in check, you can shift your focus towards other aspects of your business. You have to show your customers that you care about creating value for them, and you are not just another brand that exists out of thin air to make a quick buck. Your commitment to quality and continuous improvement will win your target customers' trust and ensure that you have healthy growth over the years.

- **Give it Time**

Last but not least, you need to manage your expectations and know that building brand trust does not happen overnight. It can take years before you can actually confirm that you have achieved the optimum brand awareness and reached your desired level of customers' trust. It is an ongoing process that will keep unraveling whenever you enter a new market, and, as your customer base widens, it will only become more complicated to manage. Keep your head in the game you are playing now and do not lose focus so you can score big.

Over the chapters in this book, you were introduced to different online and offline marketing techniques and how to use them to create your online presence. This chapter here took you further in understanding the importance of building your brand awareness and trust. You now also have, at your disposal, different tactics and strategies to enable you to build brand trust and reap the benefits that come along. Brand trust is a fragile thing that you need to handle with care so you can guarantee that your brand stays around for the long haul.

Chapter Ten: Harnessing the Power of Storytelling

The art and power of storytelling have been intrinsic to all creative arenas. Whether it's art, theatre, architecture, history, or other cultural domains, stories are a foundation of richer and deeper emotional values that one can associate with.

The potential of this tool has been realized by major companies over the years, which has made it a powerful tactic to harness any brand's identity. Followers and customers engage with a brand if their ads display stories in place of straightforward infomercials. In fact, 92% of customers want stories to be told through ads.

But how do businesses do this? And how can you incorporate effective storytelling within your marketing strategies and ads? Read on to find out.

What Exactly is Storytelling in Business Marketing?

Storytelling is a method used by marketers, public speakers, and brand communicators to stir emotion in their audiences, encourage motivation, and reinforce relatability and a deeper connection with their brand. This form of interaction with customers evokes a feeling of being related, which, in turn, produces strong emotions that urge your customers to stick to your brand name.

However, small businesses are still on the verge of realizing the power of storytelling because they believe that it is simply confined to bigger brands and names. But they are wrong. A few businesses don't incorporate storytelling within their campaigns because they don't know how to do it effectively.

What are the Benefits?

Storytelling assists brand identity in numerous ways.

• Puts you above your competitors. With persuasive storytelling, you are gaining the upper hand in marketing and thereby gaining more customers. Your future clients will notice this advancement, which will attract them towards your brand.

• It creates brand awareness. If your campaigns are influential, your brand will quickly gain recognition. Small businesses often struggle to make their mark in this competitive world and are overshadowed by gigantic names with big-budgeted marketing teams. The only way to make your way up is by anchoring your name with potent ad campaigns. Storytelling can be a major aid in cases like this.

• Increased sales and business growth. This is undeniably the biggest advantage that successful ad campaigns can bring you. As more customers are engaged, more people follow your brands, which converts leads to sales.

• Spreads your message. Your brand's motto, tag line, and beliefs are easily laid out through stories. Your company's ads are perceived with clear messages that are communicated across various channels. It provides clarity, eliminates confusion, and give your customers a reason to conduct business with you. Moreover, you can provide a sneak peek of your next project or campaign to your customers to evoke curiosity. This will compel them to stay with your brand, at least until the next project is disclosed.

All in all, if your customer likes what you do, they will spread the word further, which will multiply at an exponential rate. This will gain you more customers, more leads, more sales, more profit, and more recognition. You see, it all ties up.

How is it Used?

It all boils down to the type of audience you are entertaining. We overemphasized on the term 'target audience' throughout the book, but you must know how important it is to drive an effective marketing strategy. It's all about knowing your audience. You need to understand who they are, where they come from, and what they like or dislike. Once you are done reading this book, get to work, and build an image of your ideal client. You've already learned how to do it in the previous chapters.

Telling stories is often mistaken for direct ads, a sales pitch, your sales goal, and often boring manuscripts. It is more about team motivation, your brand identity, a resolution, a crisis, and your brand motto. In a broader sense, it is about your customers.

Any business with powerful storytelling campaigns focuses on three critical elements that form a great story, which is conflict, characters, and resolution. The character is the protagonist of any story and often relatable to the viewer or reader. The element of conflict is displayed by the character - the emotions or hardship they are going through and how their problems are typically cordial to the viewer. And the resolution, which represents the circumstances through which the character can resolve their conflict. The viewer witnesses a character development or a change of heart and instantly induces engagement and a feeling of connection.

A few other elements that complete the sphere of effective storytelling include the organization (makes the story easy to understand), entertainment (keeps the viewer engaged), and education (provides answers to various questions). Finally, the story should be universal, relatable, and memorable. By checking these boxes, you are producing a story that will leave a lasting impression on your viewers and give them enough reason to come back for more.

Effective Storytelling Techniques for Small Businesses

1. Use Stories that are Relatable

Relatable stories are a sure-fire way to capture your audience's attention. Do not make it too fictional as it will be hard for people to believe and relate to.

The most effective stories categories that tend to work include:

Success Stories

Tell a story in which you, as a small business, carved your path into this competitive world and made a niche for yourself. This also involves the success stories of people you met on the way or pointed towards someone who inspired you. But, if you constantly build your campaigns around personal rags-to-riches stories, it can get off-putting for your audience at some point. So, don't overdo it.

Failure Stories

Failure stories are a dynamic accolade to unfold all challenges and obstacles that you've been through to reach where you are today. This will demonstrate the human side of your brand. Most people can relate to failure stories (often more than success stories) as everyone has been there, and that allows you to share a comforting feeling. However, do not overemphasize your mistakes. You don't want to come across as a company that has not yet managed to put back things in order. In reality, failure stories are quite underrated, and few companies realize the impact these can bring.

Emotional Stories

Sometimes, emotional stories are more effective comparatively, especially if a viewer has been through or is passing through a similar situation. Evoking emotions in a person is the truest form of connection. Play this tip to your benefit. Many brands portray situations such as wedding proposals, the birth of a baby, and even a life-changing accident that produces a storm of emotions.

An impressive example of emotional stories in marketing campaigns can be pointed to the Philippines Levi's® brand marketing team, who came up with an emotional story plot featuring a dad and his blind son. The campaign was a shout-out for their new category of customizing clothes using an individual selection of patches, cuts, and metal studs. In the ad, the dad customizes a trucker jacket with metal studs for his son that says, "Anywhere you go, andyan lagi si papa (papa is always with you)" in braille. This ad campaign was highly applauded across the country and world, for which the marketing team also won the "Outstanding Marketing Campaign" award.

These feelings can make an emotionally packed ad campaign that can succeed if directed well.

• **Trust:** Portray a story that helps your customers to trust you. Instead of selling them a product, induce a feeling of trust, and compel them to believe that your brand is legitimate and credible. Be open and honest. This can be done by adding reviews within your ad content or personal stories of team members.

• **Happiness:** If your brand identity promotes happiness and optimism, it should show in most of your ads. Amazon constantly makes ads that generate a feeling of happiness and makes its customers smile.

• **Instant Gratification:** This produces a sense of urgency and impatience in your customers. By adding discounts or promo codes to your campaign offers, you can close multiple deals at a time.

• **Fear:** Fear is a strong emotion that might turn a customer towards you. For instance, if you are an insurance company, fear of losing your family or getting involved in an accident can urge them to take your consultation. It's certainly an evil-genius plan, but hey, it works.

These are just a few examples of how emotions can be amalgamated within your stories to make them more relatable. Other emotions, such as anger, leadership, pride, guilt, and belonging, are equally dominant.

Personalized Stories

Now, this category gets quite specific as it is targeted towards a niche audience. Personalize a story based on a person's experience, situations, or aspirations. Basically, this category is a collection of emotional, success, and failure stories that were mentioned above.

If we take an example of the current COVID-19 pandemic, most people around the world are locked at home with their families and pets. Brands are taking advantage of this situation and constructing their campaigns around these stories. This resonates well with their audience, which keeps them connected to their brand. Big names such as Honda and Emirates are creating ads that encourage people to stay home and stay safe while still posting their commercials to create awareness.

Now, this is actually inclined more towards personalizing an audience's circumstances instead of experiences. It works both ways.

2. Keep it Simple

Quite often, you need to stick to the motto 'less is more.' With increased stress and the inability to cope with work-life balance, the attention spans of most humans are growing shorter day by day. Considering this scenario, you cannot expect your customers to sit through a long ad that lasts for more than 5 minutes. Keep your campaigns short and simple. A few exceptions allow you to go beyond a certain time frame, but these are rare. Even though details are necessary to make your story pop, don't delve too deep. Some brands produce ad campaigns that last for only 30 to 40 seconds, often without any dialogue. This indicates that you don't always need illustrated lines or longer run times to explain your story. Communicating your message in a shorter and simpler manner is a challenge, but if you are successful in accomplishing this, you will be applauded.

3. Understand the Importance of Visual Storytelling

Visual storytelling is often attributed to added images within your content. Now, when we talk about storytelling, it is not just confined to ad campaigns but also to your brand's overall content. Whether it's your web page banner, an Instagram post, or simply a Google Ad, comprehend the importance of visual storytelling in all forms.

As you know, every picture tells a story. You can use a valuable piece of artwork or even a simple photograph to send your message. Hire an artist to create illustrations representing your messages or buy photographs from stock websites. Either way, make sure that a simple image spreads your motto. Visual storytelling is also important because these are instantly eye-catching when compared to simple text. Plus, your audience can instantly comprehend visuals and images when compared to plain text. So, whether it's a messaging platform, your blog, your social media channel, or a public presentation, try to incorporate visual storytelling as much as possible.

4. Use Narratives

Storytelling, if incorporated in major facets of your marketing plan, can fetch lots of attention. Here, we are talking about using narratives within your text, captions, tag lines, and quotes. We did reflect on how images are more powerful than text. But there are instances and places where you have to stick with words, such as Instagram captions. Stories are easier to grasp and interpret when compared to lessons and sayings. Let's take an example to understand this better. Instagram star and business owner, Samantha Wills, often incorporate short stories in her captions that speak of her real-life encounters. This triggers her audience to relate to her stories and circumstances, which instantly increases the value of any image.

With stories, you don't have to worry about going lengthy with your captions. Make sure that the first two to three lines are indulging, and the rest will be taken care of. You will notice yourself reading a long story caption as opposed to a long descriptive post. Another notable example is the Instagram page, Humans of New York, which is a photoblog. The page admin believes that there is a story attached to every person and being. He goes around New York and finds people that are willing to share their stories. It combines both visual and narrative storytelling. The images represent their visual emotions, and the captions explain their circumstances verbally. When combined, these are giant pieces of emotional discernment.

The point is, storytelling proves to be significant in producing emotions and prompts your audience to engage with your brand.

5. Use Stories from your Customers

What's more relatable and convincing than a fellow customer's experience with your brand. Remember the user-generated content aspect that we talked about in one of the previous chapters? This point is related to UGC. Brands like Frank Body - a brand that sells coffee scrubs, constantly post their customers' stories on their social media channels. This instigates fellow customers to buy, use, and post their stories too. You see, it can be beneficial for you in all domains.

Another benefit of using your customer stories is that you no longer have to face the pressure of constantly creating content. You can simply repost your customers' posts or tweak them to showcase creativity.

6. Consider Informational Storytelling

Now, informational storytelling is a rare occurrence that is eligible for brands that need to share descriptions or necessary information related to their products or services. For instance, law enforcement is not an easy topic for a simple man to understand with descriptive text. If you work in law, your ads can display emotional and informational stories that educate your audience through entertainment. As kids, we were told stories to filter important moral lessons. But as we grow up, we get deeper into practical understandings and no longer rely on stories. You, as a brand, need to bring this back to life.

To tell an informational story, consider the phenomenon of 'mind-meld. ' This is when a person's brain, who is also the listener, matches with your brain and style of storytelling. This occurs when your neural activities are in alignment with your audience. To incorporate this in your stories, you need to be transparent and honest with your customers. Tell them what they want to hear (ethically) and induce a feeling of trust.

If you possess the creativity, skill, and vision to use the art of storytelling, there is no better way to engage your audience. You can also hire a team of brand marketing if you lack imagination. Whichever way you choose, try telling stories and see the massive change it will make.

Chapter Eleven: 9 Guerrilla Marketing Ideas for Small Businesses

In this chapter, we will examine different marketing ideas that you can adopt for your small business that include: face-to-face marketing, social media marketing, pop up events, landscape takeover, memorable marketing, gifts, and unique infographics. The chapter begins by explaining the concept of guerrilla marketing, followed by a detailed analysis of different marketing tools that can promote your business.

What is Guerrilla Marketing?

Guerrilla marketing refers to cost-effective and innovative marketing strategies that can be utilized by small businesses that operate on a limited budget for their marketing initiatives. The term guerrilla marketing strongly borrows from the concept of guerrilla warfare, where the military often uses tactics like ambushes, raids, and surprise attacks. In marketing, the concept of guerrilla marketing uses cheap but creative strategies to draw the attention of potential clients to a certain product or service. Traditional marketing strategies are usually costly, and established businesses set substantial budgets for their marketing campaigns. This might be challenging for small businesses that are still developing.

Guerrilla marketing also allows you to take customers by surprise, and the strategy often leaves a lasting impression. This means that the strategy can be highly effective since it can appeal to the interests of many customers within a short period, which helps the organization to generate more revenue. This section outlines some of the best and cheapest guerrilla marketing ideas that you can consider for your small business. These ideas can also help you create impressive campaigns for your target audience, which can help your business to grow.

1. Face-to-Face Marketing

Face-to-face marketing is also known as personal selling, and it is a very effective tool that helps in building buyer preferences. Direct selling helps convince customers to try specific market offerings, and it can involve interaction between two or more individuals. The people involved can observe others in making decisions, and the marketer can modify their strategy to suit the needs of the customers. Personal selling also promotes the growth of long-term relationships that are good for the organization. The clients can also interact with marketers to gain more details about certain products that help them make informed decisions.

With face-to-face marketing, the customer is presented with the opportunity to listen and respond before buying a product. When a product is still new on the market, the potential clients need more information before trying it. This is when face-to-face marketing comes in handy since the customers can ask anything they want about the product. The marketer, on the other hand, gets the opportunity to convince the buyers about the benefits of purchasing the product or service.

If you are offering food and beverage products, you can set up a table in your shop where you offer the clients an opportunity to taste the product before buying it. This strategy works perfectly with alcoholic beverages like wine. Since there are numerous types of alcoholic brands available on the market, a new product is likely to generate some hype among many people. However, you need to offer them something to taste so that they can make comparisons with other types of beverages available.

Face-to-face marketing helps build confidence and trust between the company and potential customers. The other notable aspect of guerrilla marketing is that it helps marketers to connect with the "real" audience. This helps small businesses to make a lasting impression among their clients. Essentially, many businesses thrive on strong relationships with their clients, and these should be developed from the background.

2. Direct Marketing

Direct marketing is another interactive marketing strategy that does not involve face-to-face contact. Different forms of direct marketing tactics include direct mail, mobile text marketing, email marketing, or catalogs. When you use direct marketing, the message is non-public, and it is directed toward a particular person. The main advantage of direct marketing is that it is immediate, and it is also customizable. You can tailor the massage to suit your interest when you send it to your target audience. All the same, you can also prepare the message quickly so that you are able to reach many customers.

The other feature of direct marketing is that it is interactive. It allows dialogue between the marketer and the client. The marketer can also adjust the message depending on how the consumer responds. Unlike other traditional marketing methods, like advertising, which is one dimensional, direct marketing is geared towards building strong one-to-one customer relationships, which are good for business.

3. Social Media Marketing

Social media marketing is increasingly gaining widespread use among different people across the board. This marketing strategy is cost-effective, and it can reach many people. Many people use different social media platforms to engage with their friends and relatives. Enlightened businesses are also harnessing these platforms in their operations to engage with their clients. Customer engagement is very important, especially when your business is still small. Through social media, a company can roll out different marketing campaigns that are targeted at promoting product awareness among different people.

For example, a new business can use different features on media platforms like comments, likes, and clicks to reach different people. The company needs to offer marketing initiatives that are memorable so that potential customers are compelled to learn more about the offering. Guerrilla marketing is targeted communication, so it can be achieved through the use of various social media platforms. You can offer unique and creative images that make the brand stand out from the rest of the market offerings. Beautiful marketing stunts stand better chances of attracting the attention of different social media users.

The advantage of digital media is that it helps connect your brand with different people, and events become instantly viral online. Social media posts can also help create a viral effect where different users can tag their friends and relatives, which in turn promotes brand awareness among many people. This significantly bolsters your brand when many people know that it has the potential to surpass other similar offerings already existing on the market.

4. Pop-up Marketing

Pop-up marketing and flash mobs are also effective marketing strategies that can raise brand awareness. Through pop-up events, a group of marketers can randomly appear in different popular places, like shopping centers and train stations, where they physically market their brand. The strategy aims to surprise the customers, and it promotes mutual engagement with them.

In the same vein, flash mobs or roadshows also use the strategy of public appearances by a group of people who come together to showcase their product. Public performances can appeal to the interests of many people since others will only get to know about the brand during such occasions. You can incorporate your brand through face paint, T-shirts, or other signs that make it visible.

5. Well-Designed Business Cards

Attention-grabbing business cards can also go a long way in promoting your brand. Many people usually meet in different places like conferences, bars, networking events, or any other social gatherings where they get the opportunity to discuss different things. Others might ask for your business card, and they are likely to make a follow up if they find something meaningful that your business offers. A business card that is beautifully designed leaves a lasting impression, and it can go a long way in marketing your brand.

6. Outstanding Infographics

Infographics help to attract visitors to your website since they are shared on social media. Ideally, an infographic uses different forms of data to visually present a set of ideas in a captivating matter. Visual presentation of a brand is a very effective way of marketing since it gives the clients a feel of the product before they purchase it. You can choose any fun idea that is also unique that can help complement your product so that it can appeal to the emotional interests of many people. All the same, you should keep your infographics simple so that they can be easy to understand.

When you decide to use this particular strategy, make sure that the images are colorful and attractive. It is also critical to use a font that is easy to read and simple to understand. When you use visual displays, make sure that they present information about the brand so customers do not struggle to get meaning from what you will be trying to communicate.

7. Landscape Takeover

You can utilize public spaces to market your product. In urban areas, there are different landscapes that you can manipulate to market your brand. For instance, you can use bus stop ads, subway signs, and any other displays along the sidewalks. You can also think of other means of utilizing the space around your business so that it can draw the attention of passersby. For example, you can display beautiful banners around your business premises, and these can make people stop and think about the information displayed.

Additionally, you can also erect billboards around your business that can help draw the attention of potential customers.

8. Gifts

Have you ever heard about any business offering something for free? Naturally, all humans have this insatiable appetite for free things, and you can utilize this guerrilla marketing strategy to attract potential clients. Gifts to potential clients can go a long way in appealing to their interests and building a strong relationship. Many businesses have successfully utilized this guerrilla marketing tactic to attract many clients to their business. You can set up a place that you can use to give away free things to different people. You will notice that your business will attract new customers coming to get free things from your shop. Loyalty is also created when your customers know that they can get certain stuff for free.

Sales promotion is another guerrilla tactic that can help your business attract many customers. This strategy includes a wide range of tools like discounts, contests, premiums, coupons, and more. No business can escape this truism that attracting new customers is an uphill task. Therefore, it is vital to offer a variety of incentives, such as coupons and content, which allow clients to receive favorable treatment from the company.

Price discounts are very effective since they attract many people to your business. Customers are likely to switch to your brand if they know that they will get price discounts for purchasing certain products from your shop. You can extend this offer to all customers where you can say that customers get a discount after spending a certain amount in your shop. This helps to boost sales, which is good for the growth of your business.

The other advantage of sales promotion is that it invites and rewards quick responses. While the effects of this strategy may not be long-lasting like advertising, it helps attract many customers who are likely to continue buying from the shop. Many consumers are attracted by bargain deals, and the strategy can help your new business get off the ground quickly. To gain a competitive advantage, you should try to get appropriate incentives that can appeal to different individuals.

9. Public Relations

Public relations is another viable marketing strategy that is cost-effective and very believable to different readers. Public relations aims to create goodwill between the company and its publics, and this helps to promote the growth and development of business. The main advantage of public relations is that the messages reach the people as informative news instead of direct sales communication. A well-thought-out public relations campaign can be very effective since it focuses on presenting a positive image of the company.

Essentially, the strategy of public relations also aims at creating mutual relationships between the company and the clients. As you are now aware, the success of the company strongly depends on the quality of the relationships it has with the customers. While some people use public relations as an afterthought, the truth is that it plays a significant role in presenting a positive image of the firm. When the company gains the trust of the clients, it can positively respond to their needs since they will be open about their expectations from the business.

The other thing about PR is that it is economical and ideal for small businesses that do not have strong marketing budgets. It uses a storytelling strategy to send information about the company and products that a company offers. A PR campaign can be achieved through the use of different media. Community newspapers and radio are good channels that can help different companies disseminate information about their products to different people. When people first read about the brand in the press, the next they will do is to take action. They will make a decision based on the information they have about the product.

Advantages of Guerrilla Marketing

When your business is still small, it does not have huge operating capital like other established businesses. Therefore, small businesses may not be able to fund expensive marketing campaigns, as big companies can. However, you can consider guerrilla marketing tactics since they are the best alternative to conventional marketing strategies that require strong sponsorship. The primary advantage of guerrilla marketing is that it is budget-friendly, and it is ideal for small businesses. When your company is small, it might be challenging to allocate a large marketing budget like what other established organizations do. Guerrilla marketing is an effective tool that can help the company generate an impressive return on investment if properly used.

Stronger Brand Identity

The Guerrilla marketing tactic helps the business to build a stronger brand identity, which, in turn, also gives it a competitive advantage. The strategy helps the company to reflect on how its new product will challenge the existing products by offering new features and benefits. The tactic also allows customers to judge the new offering to establish if it can satisfy their needs.

Marketing plays a crucial role in raising brand awareness among different customers. It also helps attract potential clients to the product offered, which helps promote the growth of the business. However, marketing can be a costly undertaking, especially for small businesses that are still new in the industry. Paid forms of marketing, like advertising and sponsorship, can be expensive to many small businesses that are still growing. All the same, other economic marketing strategies can be adopted by small businesses like guerrilla marketing tactics.

As discussed in this chapter, guerrilla marketing ideas for small businesses are cost-effective, and they can significantly help your business attract many customers. These tactics help marketers present their products to different clients through interactive methods. This approach to business is effective since it helps marketers to engage with the customers in a meaningful way. The clients can also ask the marketers some pertinent questions about the brand, which helps them make informed decisions. Along with being cost-effective, guerrilla marketing also leaves a lasting impression among the consumers if properly executed.

Chapter Twelve: 10 Small Business Branding Trends to Look Out For

With the immense rise in competition, brands are constantly evolving and introducing new trends to stand out and build recognition. These trends can also be attributed to the rise in technological advancements and consistent innovation.

In the past, branding trends were simply confined to visual representation, which has massively changed today. It's more than just a catchy brand name and an attractive logo. Visual representation is certainly important, but brands are nowadays looking beyond this and tapping into customer satisfaction, social consciousness, and improved interaction.

We already learned what branding is and what you can do to create a unique brand identity in one of the previous chapters. To be more specific, we are going to throw light on modern branding trends and how these can be used to shift your brand identity to enhance awareness, recognition, and engagement.

Modern branding trends also imply the basic necessities in branding. To begin with, you need a name that will resonate with your brand identity and is easy for customers to remember. Try to play with it a bit and ideate something unique (creative and easy). Shorter but catchy brand names are the new trend. Don't forget the logo. A simple and minimal logo is highly appreciated. To complete the basic set of branding, choose a color palette that comprises not more than two colors.

To give you an idea of other branding trends in-depth, this chapter has curated 10 such effective strategies. Read on to know more.

1. Inclusivity and Diversity

As we mentioned, brands are much more than colorful logos and fancy names. Customers are sub-consciously expecting more with each passing day. These expectations are also partly because of the struggles and everyday hustle that has led human beings wanting more. Societal aspects, such as body positivity and diversity, are no longer confined to human discussions and taboo subjects. These are also increasingly reflecting on people's consumer habits, which is why brands are incorporating inclusivity and diversity within their strategies for their customers to relate to their philosophies. In fact, 70% of consumers today would choose a brand that is diverse and inclusive.

Brands such as Dove and Fenty Beauty showcase an identity that resonates with a woman's real beauty, compelling women customers to acknowledge self-love and appreciate who they are. Their beauty campaigns refrain from spreading picture-perfect slim models and instead display a caricature of the real woman through aspects revolving around age, nationality, race, ethnicity, and gender orientation. Customers realize this new-age era that breaks beauty stereotypes and is ready to accept brands a heartbeat. This is just an example. Brands are also addressing other social norms such as domestic violence, mental health issues, and differently-abled people. It depends on what kind of customers your brand caters to and the type of products or services.

However, do not incorporate such values if you don't believe in them. Your brand is a reflection of you and your beliefs and vice-versa. Standing up for something you don't believe is simply betraying your customers.

2. Tech-Induced

With the advancements in technology, a number of brands are incorporating artificial intelligence and chatbots within several domains, such as customer support and conversational marketing. As we know now, interaction is necessary to keep customers engaged. And customer satisfaction tops it all. At times, with a small team, it's impossible to solve every inquiry or reply to every email or direct message. This is when technology can help you out. Employing people to solve every kind of query can cost you more. Since most customers prefer to solve their queries through texts and online chats instead of phone calls, you can gladly use chatbots to resolve customer issues at a much lesser price.

Similar technological additions are not only useful for customer interaction but also build awareness, automation, development, and customer loyalty by a wider margin. Along with chatbots and automated voice assistants, you can implement other technological operations such as mobile applications, augmented reality, and virtual reality. Since most users prefer operating social media and web pages through their cell phones, you get a massive potential to create augmented experiences for your audience. Incorporation of technology within your strategies will enhance customer services, help meet further customer demands, and allow you to fetch user data.

3. The Surge in Online Communities

We've been repeating over and over how engagement and interaction are important to keep your customers attached to your brand. Online communities are a new trend among brands. These communities are open forums for customers to ask questions, speak their minds, and discuss important subjects of interest. With online communities, brands are more inclined towards providing better customer experience and satisfaction instead of selling products. By doing so, they are automatically turning their leads into sales. Many platforms also occasionally offer exclusive tips and advice from experts within their discipline.

Brands are also increasingly learning about their customer's needs and fetching valuable feedback to improve their products. For example, Sephora hosts an online community known as the Beauty Insider Community. This forum encourages its customers to share tips, beauty product reviews, beauty hacks, personal experiences, current trends, and overall suggestions. These topics of discussions are segregated into categories, and customers can choose whether they want to join a live chat, get inspiration, ask questions, or talk about beauty concerns. The concerned interfaces are usually aesthetically appealing to lure customers to join these groups. You can begin by adding customers on social media groups and slowly taking it to personalized forums.

4. 'Phigital' Customer Experiences

Phigital comes from physical plus digital, which has taken the branding world by storm. It's the best of both worlds. With phigital customer experiences, your clients can know your brand and your products in a wider sense. This is not only useful for your brand's development but has a higher success rate of turning leads into sales. Brands combine physical presence with digital tools such as AR. For example, Audi's showroom in London displays a touchscreen that uses augmented reality to show the features of a car before actually seeing or getting into the actual car. It not only saves time for customers and dealers but helps the customer make informed decisions. Your brand is surely receiving engagement, along with an establishment of a trusting bonding.

Incorporation of phigital experiences will set you apart and raise you above your competitor's spot in the market. You can also take inspiration from McDonald's Pick N Play billboard game that was first introduced in one of Stockholm's branches. This allowed customers to play the game on the billboard directly using their cell phones without having to download an app. They could do it by opening the website mentioned on the billboard, turning on GPS, and scoring points. The user that stayed alive for 30 seconds could win a free meal. This attracted a lot of customers to their branch, eventually resulting in higher sales.

5. Eco-Friendly or Sustainable Norms

With the rise of harmful emissions, the use of plastic, and increased carbon footprint, the world is facing a climate crisis. And it is partly due to the products we consume. If brands start acting wisely and incorporate eco-friendly and conscious decisions within their paradigm, the world will surely become a better place. In fact, 88% of customers believe that the climatic changes will massively reverse if all brands start making conscious decisions. Even though adopting sustainable approaches are a bit more expensive, you can always recover them by increasing your prices. 61% of millennials and 58% of the Gen-Z population are willing to purchase sustainable products, even if they cost more.

Even if your products don't align with sustainable norms, try to keep your packaging legitimate and avoid the use of plastic. This is a tiny yet significant step that will be greatly appreciated by your customers. And, if you look at it in a broader sense, you are impacting the environment given the number of customers you serve annually. It will surely make an impact in the long run. One such example of a brand that adopted eco-friendly production is Patagonia, which is on its way to create sustainable outdoor gear and apparel.

6. Tweaks in Logos

Many brands, such as Ikea, Coca Cola, and Nike, have adapted to newer versions of their iconic logos. While some of these are slight tweaks, most of them are adapted into minimal versions of respective logo designs without losing their significance. These designs still resonate with customers, and they can instantly recognize the brands despite the changes. The main factors behind this lingering recognition are the form and color palette that create any brand's identity. Some companies have longer brand names, which make it a necessity to shorten or revamp their logos to attach on social media channels, documents, and sites that demand different logo layouts.

Another benefit of tweaking logos is to provide visual variety. Since customers are quite accustomed to seeing the same version of any brand image day in and out, a slightly altered logo provides a change in perception. Plus, your brand comes across as a risk-taker that is open to some changes. The logos usually vary in complexity, size, and even color. The concept of minimalism is profoundly expanding, especially within marketing and branding disciplines. Brands are using this concept to shape-shift their logos, which has had a successful outcome.

7. Your Brand's Hashtags

Official hashtags are a thing now. Many brands are coming up with their own hashtags that are used all over their social media channels, websites, and campaigns. It is typically dedicated to social media platforms that use hashtags to categorize content, such as Instagram and Twitter. It not only enables a user to find a particular brand with ease but also creates recognition. Along with inducing brand awareness, customer engagement was noted to increase by a whopping 50%, which is a major outcome for any brand. In other words, a specific set of hashtags have the power to finally offer a position in this saturated market. Plus, you can monitor your brand's ranking and reputation in the eyes of your customers.

You can create your own hashtags either by shortening your brand's name or coming up with a short brand motto. Use these hashtags in your captions and urge your followers to use it when they purchase your product and post it on social media. Other ways of building recognition with hashtags are by reposting your customer's experiences and user-generated content and running contests that offer a brief of using hashtags. An elite example of an official hashtag is #essielove, which belongs to the nail polish brand, Essie.

8. Anti-Ad Tactics

Now, this is some kind of reverse psychology that tends to work (at least with the brands that tried it and were by far successful). Ads have become a nonsensical distraction that flood social media channels, web pages, and even places surrounding your daily commute. The ad market is saturated at such a level that most people ignore them, which makes them useless. Companies spend hundreds of dollars to print posters or flyers and promote ads online, which is all in vain. So, what can be done to stand out and actually trigger people to notice your ads?

Brands have come up with an anti-ad campaign that actually leads people to not see their ads, which builds curiosity, and they eventually end up acknowledging their ads. Let's take an example to make it simpler. Doritos deleted their brand name and logo on social media to prove that their customers would still recognize them, which they did. It was a big risk but eventually was a massive success. Similarly, dating app Hinge encouraged their users to delete their app, declaring that you will eventually find an ideal partner through this app, which is why you won't need it anymore. One thing you must keep in mind is that these anti-ad tactics work only with big brand names because these are well-known. Small businesses should refrain from such tactics as they first need to build recognition and a customer base.

9. Authenticity and Honesty

Falling along the lines of inclusivity, brands also need to be more authentic and honest with their customers. This realization has developed into a current trend that focuses on providing a brand's most authentic side through their campaigns. Popular brands have made authenticity a permanent feat while promoting their campaigns. This trend also emerged because customer trust was rapidly declining with every passing year, and only 34% of customers trusted their brands. In fact, 90% of millennials would buy from brands that are more real, honest, and organic when compared to products that are more aesthetically oriented and 'perfect.'

Authentic ads refrain from using flawless models and Photoshopped editorials in their ad campaigns. They show sincere content that is more substantial and contains more substance. There is hardly any pressure to buy from these kinds of brands, which portrays an idea of affiliation instead of commercialism. Take the example of McDonald's. To show transparency and clarity, the brand floated a behind-the-scenes video that resolved rumors regarding negative food ingredients. The brand was open and ready to provide all answers that surrounded their food, and the campaign was named "Our Food, Your Questions." Such videos and content show the real manufacturing processes along with the quality of materials or ingredients you use, urging your customers to trust you.

If you are a new business, you are in luck because you can begin promoting your brand that revolves around authenticity from the very beginning.

10. Triggering Nostalgic Feelings

In a previous chapter that focused on effective storytelling, we learned how emotions are necessary to trigger a customer's emotions and induce a connection with your brand. Well, what's a better trigger than nostalgia? Childhood memories serve as a testimonial for a happy and carefree period, which is quite precious for most of us. Whether it's music, food, books, fashion, an image, or something representation of previous days, you can induce an emotional experience. Some brands were recently inspired by this ploy and decided to incorporate it into their campaigns. One such notable example is Spotify. This music app dug out old habits and music from the '80s and '90s and compared them to the latest trends. The brand added them in its new campaigns that became extremely popular in 2019.

By exploring your customer's positive emotions, you can have a better chance at engagement, leading to forming a trusted connection. And we know that trust is important for a positive outcome. So, if you are exploring your options and looking for a twist, consider a 'blast from the past' campaign and apply a set of objectives that align with your brand message.

These are some of the current branding trends that you should definitely include in your strategies and implement them at some point. They will set you apart from your competitors and build an authoritative image in your customers' minds. Modern customers and consumers are looking for variation, which can be provided through branding trends.

Conclusion

Whether you're a small business owner, in charge of branding, an influencer, an entrepreneur, or a motivational speaker, you'll find the various branding strategies and tactics mentioned in this book of great use. Branding has always revolved around foundational concepts that can easily evolve into different streams.

This handy book can be the best ally in your branding journey. From versatile strategies to tips, you'll be able to get the most out of what branding has to offer. It's not odd to find some branding techniques mentioned a bit hard to implement at first, as they may require a different environment. But you can be assured that you'll be able to find the best techniques that suit your need.

The branding concepts mentioned are proven and updated, with no over-the-top business maneuvers that could put your business at risk. None of the techniques are random; they are explained in detail to provide you with enough information that allows you to judge whether it will be beneficial for you or not.

After reading this book, you'll be able to easily identify the branding strategies of different brands just by looking at them. To put it simply, a brand is how the image of the product you sell is perceived; branding is the marketing strategy you can use to shape that image.

In the end, it's up to you to define your company's mission, core values, the benefits you provide to consumers, and the qualities you care about portraying the most. As long as you're able to figure out the requirements for creating a great brand image, you're on your way to figuring out the perfect branding strategies for you.

While this book will provide more than enough strategies and techniques, you should research as much as you can, your consumers' needs, and your plans for the future. Sustainable brand growth requires having a vision and mission that acts as a compass for your business.

Branding can be thought of as a set of moves that can create cultural relevance, and cultural relevance is essential in breaking through the noise generated by hundreds of brands in any industry. The digital branding techniques are your greatest tools in producing the loudest buzz to provide a cultural breakthrough.

It's not uncommon for brands to stumble on their way to becoming as relevant with the audience as possible, but some setbacks can take a long time to recover from. This is why you should not randomly choose some of the branding techniques in this book without making sure that they'll be the most beneficial for your business. A brand should never appear inconsistent or over-reaching with their branding efforts.

Hopefully, completing this book will mean that you've crossed a great barrier in the art of branding. This doesn't mean that you've suddenly become the master of the branding domain, but it can mean that you're on your way to craft and develop great branding strategies that incorporate different elements, which will grow your business and help you to succeed.

References

https://www.brandingmag.com/2015/10/14/what-is-branding-and-why-is-it-important-for-your-business/

https://www.entrepreneur.com/article/313369

https://strategynewmedia.com/why-is-branding-important/

https://www.forbes.com/sites/marketshare/2012/05/27/why-brand-building-is-important/#4ed4286e3006

https://blog.markgrowth.com/knowing-your-audience-is-critical-to-your-brand-eb02c0ffc912 https://blog.hootsuite.com/target-market/

https://www.workhorsemkt.com/understanding-brand-audience/, https://www.youtube.com/watch?v=gct8EfbkI0E

https://blog.hubspot.com/marketing/online-presence

https://www.allbusiness.com/5-reasons-online-presence-essential-small-businesses-106737-1.html/2

https://blog.givingassistant.org/brands-that-give-back/

https://www.forbes.com/sites/forbestechcouncil/2018/04/20/how-to-create-a-big-online-presence-for-your-small-business/#6913c2836c34

https://www.reviewtrackers.com/blog/brand-trust/

https://belmarx.com/brand-awareness-for-small-business/

https://www.entrepreneur.com/article/289167

https://bloggingwizard.com/social-media-marketing-tips/

https://www.quicksprout.com/social-media-for-small-business/

https://www.youtube.com/watch?v=3fgQN8upYik

https://ied.eu/project-updates/service-branding-vs-product-branding/
https://aventivestudio.com/branding-products-vs-branding-services/
https://yourbusiness.azcentral.com/advantages-product-branding-8115.html https://smallbusiness.chron.com/branding-services-41986.html

https://blog.hubspot.com/blog/tabid/6307/bid/31739/7-components-that-comprise-a-comprehensive-brand-strategy.aspx

https://cmgpartners.com/blog/branding-marketing-strategies/
https://www.columnfivemedia.com/how-to-create-a-brand-strategy

http://www.creativeguerrillamarketing.com/guerrilla-marketing/guerrilla-marketing-works-small-businesses/

https://www.youtube.com/watch?v=FTK4m040whA

https://www.youtube.com/watch?v=qtp5eZhdlYA

https://www.hatchbuck.com/blog/guerrilla-marketing-small-business/

https://financesonline.com/branding-trends/

https://www.lyfemarketing.com/blog/branding-trends/

https://www.thebalancesmb.com/brand-identity-and-marketing-2295442

https://www.feedough.com/brand-image-explanation-examples/

https://www.qualtrics.com/experience-management/product/create-buyer-persona/

https://www.qualtrics.com/experience-management/product/concept-testing-questions/

https://www.qualtrics.com/blog/brand-positioning/

https://www.forbes.com/sites/forbesagencycouncil/2016/10/31/why-brand-image-matters-more-than-you-think/#7bf8769110b8

https://www.columnfivemedia.com/how-to-create-a-brand-identity

https://www.thebalancesmb.com/define-your-brand-identity-2294834

Here's another book by Chase Barlow
that you might be interested in

INSTAGRAM
MARKETING

Unlock the Secrets to Using this Social Media Platform for
Personal Branding, Growing Your Small Business and
Connecting with Influencers Who Will Grow Your Brand

CHASE BARLOW

CPSIA information can be obtained
at www.ICGtesting.com
Printed in the USA
LVHW020012050820
662290LV00016B/340